30 DAYS for THE LIFE you PRAYED for

30 DAYS IN CHRIST

by Edward Venters

A wholly owned subsidiary of **TBN**

30 Days for the Life You Prayed For

Trilogy Christian Publishers
A Wholly Owned Subsidiary of Trinity Broadcasting Network
2442 Michelle Drive
Tustin, CA 92780

Copyright © 2021 by Edward Venters

Manufactured in the United States of America
10 9 8 7 6 5 4 3 2 1
Library of Congress Cataloging-in-Publication Data is available.

ISBN: 978-1-63769-462-6
E-ISBN: 978-1-63769-463-3

DEDICATION

This book is dedicated to my late friend, Gerald Howse, who, every step of the way, believed in me and encouraged me to be the man I aspired to be. Thank you, my friend, for always being a phone call away and always being willing to listen and pray.

TABLE OF CONTENTS

FOREWORD

You have a treasure in your hands. Why is it a treasure? Because it will lead you to destinations of peace, calm, and freedom. As we know, to become what you have never been, you must do what you have never done. In my practice as a naturopathic doctor, as well as in ministry, I see the greatest struggles with people not being able to maintain consistency. This would include the areas of diet, sleep, exercise, reading habits, and spending quality time with God. It takes consistency to build habits. Obviously, we see that you can be consistent and create either bad habits or healthy habits.

As I have read this book by my personal friend Edward, I can absolutely tell you that going through thirty days without wavering is one of the most constructive things you can do. Each day you spend time reading these words, you will have scripture and goals upon which to meditate. This is the beginning of great things for you.

Don't put this book down. Finish it. Commit right now to this endeavor, and, without question, you will see your life actually become your best life.

—Dr. Mark Sherwood,
Author, ND

INTRODUCTION

If you're reading this book, you are looking for a change and you've tried to set goals in the past, yet you keep coming up short. Maybe you want to go to a new level in your personal or business life. That's good; change is not a bad thing. In fact, it's a part of growth. In order for something to grow, it has to evolve, like the all-so-beautiful caterpillar.

I'm sure you're thinking, *He meant butterfly, right?*

In fact, I didn't. The caterpillar is beautiful because it initiated the first phase of metamorphosis, and in return, it evolved into a butterfly. Everything about the caterpillar looks different, but I can assure you it is the same organism. So, are you the caterpillar figuratively and literally? If this resonates with you, this book is for you. We are going to take your goals, which together form your vision or purpose, and mix them with the Word of God and change our lives from this day forward.

Are you ready? I'm asking you to devote thirty days to yourself and accomplishing your goals. This journey will not be like any other, and with the help from the Holy Spirit, you will become one step closer to the man or woman God intended you to be. So, with this journey, you are going to create, execute, and establish a new lifestyle all through the Word of God!

So, let's get started. The first things you need are the items on the following page. This is the fun part because you are going to create and speak life into yourself.

1. The Holy Bible.
2. Markers or pens—no pencils because whatever we write will be established.
3. Poster board or standard US paper (8.5" x11").
4. Magazine or something that you cut out to make a vision board.

One final note before you get started: feel free to share your thoughts, prayers, and experience working through this book on social media; use the hashtag #30DaysInChrist to connect with myself and other readers.

DAY 1

SCRIPTURES

"Then the LORD answered me and said: 'Write the vision and make it plain on tablets, that he may run who reads it.'"

— Habakkuk 2:2 (NKJV)

"If you really fulfill the royal law according to the Scripture, 'You shall love your neighbor as yourself,' you do well."

— James 2:8 (NKJV)

"The steps of a man are established by the LORD, when he delights in his way."

— Psalm 37:23 (ESV)

The steps that we are going to take are simple but powerful. The first thing we are going to do is pray and ask the Holy Spirit to lead us in configuring our goals. Next, take a few moments and pray that the Lord leads you in the direction that He has already planned for you (Psalm 37:23).

Your life was predestined before the stars were created and the mountains peaked. God loves you so much that He gave you a piece of Him to create and speak, just like He did in Genesis 1.

Writing and speaking goals is a game-changer. When you begin to write down your vision, you allow yourself to see what it is you're creating your life to be (Habakkuk 2:2). You were created to create. This is our nature and our essence. When you were a kid, you had this God-given skill. We call it imagination. As we begin to get older, life happens, and we lose a little of our imagination. Trials and tribulations set in; reality begins to shake up what we thought was real. Society tells us to fall in line with the in-crowd and fit in, but God created us to be set apart (Psalm 4:3).

So, write the goals and vision and make it plain so that you can understand them. Each thing you list must fall in line with the Word of God. After you have written the goals and vision, the next step is prayer. I hope you see a consistent trend in our new lifestyle. It consists of prayer and the Word of God. Smith Wigglesworth says, "We must be taken out of the ordinary. We must be brought into the extraordinary. We must live in a glorious position, over the flesh and the devil, and everything of the world. God has ordained us, clothed us within, and manifested upon us His glory that we may be the sons with promise of Son-likeness to Him."

Now, after you have created this goal sheet, you need to hang it in a place that you will always see every day. No excuses and no turning back from this point. I hope you're ready for the life that God has planned for you. From this day forward, you are a new creature in Christ.

DAY 2

SCRIPTURES

"When I was a child, I spoke as a child, I understood as a child, I thought as a child; but when I became a man, I put away childish things."

— 1 Corinthians 13:11 (NKJV)

"And He called the twelve together and gave them power and authority over all the demons and to heal diseases."

— Luke 9:1 (NASB)

"Be careful what you be, because a time will come you can't be what you want to be, because of what you've been"

— Apostle Ron Venters Sr.

―――――――――――――――

As far back as I can remember, my grandfather has spoken these words to me. He challenged me to make the right decision and always do the right thing. Today is going to be a self-reflection segment. We will have these periodically throughout the thirty days. This will be a critical time to understand yourself. The current place you're in is because of your actions for however long you've been accountable for your own well-being.

Some call it the butterfly effect: every action has a reaction or consequence; "We reap what we sow." Ralph Waldo Emerson said the Law of Cause and Effect is the "law of laws." So, what has gotten you here to this point in your life? What are some key decisions you have made? What are some daily decisions you make that are futile or non-conducive to bettering yourself? We want to eventually eradicate these wasteful actions, but first, we have to be able to identify them (1 Corinthians 13:11). Each decision we make matters, the biggest lie the devil can tell you is that it's okay, one time won't hurt, or just a little never hurt anyone. Be clear on the fact that the enemy manipulates and coerces us into sin. We have to identify this and speak against it. Controlling your thought life is the key to a disciple (disciplined) lifestyle. We, as humans, have only so much willpower. We have a sin nature, but once we implement Christ, He gives us authority over everything the devil throws at us (Luke 9:1).

Now write down some things that you know are wasteful. Maybe sitting on the phone with your friends or watching too much of that TV show. Only you and the Holy Spirit know what is unnecessary in your current life. If you don't know or can't recognize these traits, pray and ask the Holy Spirit for guidance. He will "direct your paths." The Bible clearly tells us this and makes it a promise.

John 16:13 (NKJV) says, "However, when He, the Spirit of truth, has come, He will guide you into all truth; for He will not speak on His own authority, but whatever He hears He will speak; and He will tell you things to come."

DAY 3

SCRIPTURES

"Death and life are in the power of the tongue, and those who love it will eat its fruit."

— Proverbs 18:21 (NKJV)

"Let no corrupting talk come out of your mouths, but only such as is good for building up, as fits the occasion, that it may give grace to those who hear."

— Ephesians 4:29 (ESV)

The most important rule you could ever go by from this day forward is, "watch your mouth!" Your mouth is the pilot for your destiny, and it is the carburetor for igniting your journey. You are in the infancy stage of your journey, and the new goals and Holy Ghost-inspired path you are on are very fragile. So that means watching what you say; your words carry truth and revelation. They can be viewed as a bullet in a gun, though we tend to take a weapon more serious than our own mouths, the truth is they're the same. As soon as you speak negative into the atmosphere, it travels to its resting place. Let's take into consideration Genesis 1:2-5 (ESV), which says:

The earth was without form and void, and darkness was over the face of the deep. And the Spirit of God was hovering over the face of the waters. And God said, "Let there be light," and there was light. And God saw that the light was good. And God separated the light from the darkness. God called the light Day, and the darkness he called Night. And there was evening and there was morning, the first day...

Let's focus on two major points in this passage. The first, "was without form and void," means nothing existed in this space. Not until God spoke was there change to this dimension and an immediate change happened. Some scholars say it took millions, even billions of years, for the earth to form. This doesn't seem to be the case, if we base creation from the Bible and of God, we know it was immediate; when He speaks, things move. When God speaks, there is no delay, especially with nature and inanimate objects. They have no choice but to get in line with the Word of God. So, as we stated in yesterday's message, we have God inside of us. If He is in us and His power dwells within us, then that means what we say should happen immediately in theory.

There's just one thing this all falls back on: our level of faith, which is the force in the spirit realm that moves God. Jesus says in Matthew (NKJV), "Because of your unbelief; for assuredly, I say to you, if you have faith as a mustard seed, you will say to this mountain, 'Move from here to there,' and it will move; and nothing will be impossible for you."

We will discuss the "let there be light" in tomorrow's chapter. Take a note; from this day forward, you will watch your mouth and the things you speak.

DAY 4

SCRIPTURES

The earth was without form and void, and darkness was over the face of the deep. And the Spirit of God was hovering over the face of the waters. And God said, "Let there be light," and there was light. And God saw that the light was good. And God separated the light from the darkness. God called the light Day, and the darkness he called Night. And there was evening and there was morning, the first day...

— Genesis 1:2-5 (ESV)

Holy Ghost-inspired living is the key. That is a thought life that constantly reflects the Word of God. We, as Christians, tend to separate our habits or hobbies from the church and the Word. This should not be the case. Every aspect of our life should revolve around the Word of God. No matter what we do, we should be caught glorifying God with our entire lives. This includes eating habits, friends, entertainment, music, movies, etc.

In order for us to break this cycle, there has to be a cadence spoken. When I played football, the coach would give us cadences that would dictate the current play and scheme depending upon the opposing offense. We would try and predict the play they were going to run based on previous games and films we studied. Most coaches only have a handful of plays, and, especially in high school, they tend to be fairly simple. So, we would prepare three plays for one occasion, and if their offense shifted like we predicted, we would shift the defense so that would better prepare us for the plays they ran. This is the same case with old habits and fighting the devil. The Word of God is our coach, and whatever the devil throws at us, we have a book full of audibles designed to defeat any and everything he throws at us. Life and death should be spoken into our current circumstances.

Remember the Genesis account? We are going to pair this with Proverbs 18:21. We tend to have a negative association with death. Not in this case. We are going to speak death upon our old habits and our old thought life. In order for a new life to be birthed, the old must die (2 Corinthians 5:17).

So, when that old habit tries to come back to life, we must say, "I rebuke that in the name of Jesus!"

DAY 5

SCRIPTURES

"If you really fulfill the royal law according to the Scripture, 'You shall love your neighbor as yourself,' you do well."

— James 2:8

"And if children, then heirs—heirs of God and joint-heirs with Christ, if indeed we suffer with Him, that we may also be glorified together."

— Romans 8:17

What do we accomplish by staying the same, year after year and month after month? Our purpose in this life is to grow, to increase the kingdom of God. Is there purpose in your current life? God wants you to grow. God wants more from you. Your life as an ambassador of Christ is supposed to be abundant. You owe God that much; you owe your neighbor that much. If you can't find purpose or motivation, then inspiring the next person should motivate you. There are people who need a hero. They need a champion. Loving my neighbor as I love myself usually becomes associated with being nice or caring for them. I believe this is true, but it also should be inspiring them by our lives to live for Christ.

I remember when I was in middle school playing football, we would practice across the street from the high school team. They were nationally ranked at the time, and they had a few blue-chip all-American guys that were nothing shy of spectacular. We could hear the excitement and the intensity across the street. They were bigger and faster than us at the time. They seemed like heroes to a degree. It was the big stage, the lights, the fans, and cheerleaders… Going to the games and watching the community cheer them on inspired me to want to be on that level. I aimed to be a part of the glory of a Muskogee Roughers; the chance of being a part of the LOD defense (Legion of Doom) was my goal. This was only the case because of the attitude they carried. There was a certain mystique about being a part of a hard-nose defense. We were tough and would hurt anyone that played against us.

This should be true about our lives as Christians (not hurting anyone); we are heirs to the Throne of God. We are to walk in favor and grace everywhere we go. We should inspire people to be like us. This will give us a chance to give God the glory. He is worthy to be praised, and He is worthy to live for. Make sure that you are the light wherever you set foot and that you are a great ambassador for Christ!

DAY 6

SCRIPTURES

"Two are better than one, because they have a good return for their labor: If either of them falls down, one can help the other up. But pity anyone who falls and has no one to help them up."

— Ecclesiastes 4:9-12

"A man who has friends must himself be friendly, but there is a friend who sticks closer than a brother."

— Proverbs 18:24

Support is key in the process of changing your life. Surrounding yourself with people that love you and care for you is essential. There is always someone who is willing to help you. I know there are cases where you might not have a family or did not grow up in a healthy environment. This is totally understandable, but as you grow towards Christ, He will gravitate the right people toward your life. It is ideal that you find someone who will help you grow in Christ and in life.

The writer of Ecclesiastes says that two are better than one because if one falls, the other is there to pick them up. When you feel like caving in and giving up, having someone to lean on can make all the difference.

God intended for us to have companions. He clearly stated this in Genesis. Adam had the world at his fingertips and even had animal friends. Even greater, he had God right there with him. So, there must have been something else that God or even the animals couldn't offer him. You would think that if you literally walked with God, it would be enough, but Adam clearly wasn't happy. Having a strong friend and companion can make the difference in your life. Eve was Adam's friend and lover; she was to help him fulfill the assignment that God placed before him. Adam didn't know what he needed. At that time, he was the only human that walked the earth that we know of, but God knew. God knew when the right time was, and He knew exactly what Adam needed to fulfill his destiny. God knew Jesus was to enter into the earth from the beginning. He knew His creation would need help.

He loved us so much that He had a provisional plan in place so that His so beloved creation would not perish. That's how much He loves us. He created us knowing we'd sin, knowing we'd spit in His face, but yet He carried out His plan and gave Himself in human form so that we would have salvation because of His death and resurrection. By faith, we gained the ultimate companion, the Holy Spirit. He is our guide, our helper, and while you're waiting on your physical companion, lean on Jesus. He will direct your paths and make them straight.

DAY 7

SCRIPTURES

"I press toward the mark for the prize of the high calling of God in Christ Jesus."

— Philippians 3:14

Hallelujah! Today marks seven days of focus, determination, faith, and persistence. Most people say you should reward yourself. Not us; we are different. We are going to push harder and become even more disciplined and more determined. We are going to crush our goals and what's coming next for the rest of the journey. Let's shorten our time watching TV or reduce something out of our diet. We can do whatever we put our minds to. Maybe save a little extra out of our next paycheck. Whatever you decide to make a commitment to…crush that goal. This is your new lifestyle, your new life!

Take some time to think about the last seven days. Only you know what you could have done better. Write it below, and we will revisit this page in the future. Be strict on yourself. Take no breaks on improving yourself.

Lastly, after you have written those old things down, repeat this prayer:

"Heavenly Father, I come in the name of Jesus, asking you to help me, strengthen me, draw me closer to my destiny. Draw me closer to be the woman/man you created me to be. Holy Spirit, fill me, inspire my living, my eating habits, my daily walk. Less of me and more of you, the old me is dead, and the new me is here. I thank you for the blood and the opportunity to better myself, and I will give you the glory in the end. In the name of Jesus, I pray. Amen!"

Now write the vision and make it plain in the name of Jesus. Make it happen!

DAY 8

SCRIPTURES

"Consider it pure joy, my brothers, when you encounter trials of many kinds, because you know that the testing of your faith develops perseverance. Allow perseverance to finish its work, so that you may be mature and complete, not lacking anything."

— James 1:2-4

As we walk life and grow deeper in self and in spirit, we will overcome many petty trials.

I remember I had such a difficult time keeping my room clean. I would make excuses for not making my bed up or not stacking my shoes. My favorite lines were, "Practice takes all my energy," or "I'm just going to get back in the bed later on. Why waste time making the bed?" There was always a reason as to why my room was dirty. The older I got, the more it became a problem. Going to college and having roommates began to shed light on my habits of filth.

I think the most embarrassing moment was having an old friend visit me, and I couldn't take them into my room because it had a stench that was unpleasant. (Hey, that was the old me. Let's be clear, I would clean up if I entertained a lady or if I knew company was coming.) So, as I said, it became very bothersome because of not keeping my room clean.

Being undisciplined started carrying over to other things. My car was dirty. I would go in public, and my clothes would have spots because I put clean clothes in the dirty clothes basket. How could something so private be a catalyst for everything else? Well, because it reflected my thought process; allowing chaos in one aspect of my life allowed it to seep into other parts of my life. I had to have an epiphany to realize what I had allowed to go on.

How did I change this phase of my life? Simply by stacking my shoes. Regardless of whether I made my bed, I began to stack my shoes every day. I would even stack the same pair in the same spot, never switching spots or stacking in another location. I began to build discipline by conquering one task. Then that led to making my bed, which led to putting clothes in a basket, which eliminated the odors. This was a domino effect that developed into a lifestyle. I can't remember the last time I didn't make my bed or stack my shoes. The simple act of stacking my shoes gave me the discipline to do everything else.

This is how our journey of growth is. It's like the ancient proverb on how to eat an elephant: one bite at a time. Not only is it impossible to eat an elephant in one bite, but it's also not practical. So, keep conquering the small tasks in your life, strive to be excellent in every area of your life. This will carry over to creating the life you prayed for.

DAY 9

SCRIPTURES

"And we know that all things work together for good to those who love God, to those who are the called according to His purpose."

— Romans 8:28 (NKJV)

"Can a man hide himself in secret places so that I cannot see him? declares the Lord. Do I not fill heaven and earth? declares the Lord."

— Jeremiah 23:24 (ESV)

Being thankful goes a long way; be thankful for the journey. You should be elated for where you are in life right now. You should be highly excited about what the Lord is doing right now. The dedication you are giving right now will pay off. Nothing that you are doing is in vain. Remember that everything matters (Romans 8:28).

That is even true with your failures. God calculated and made a way for you. Jeremiah 23:24 (ESV) says, "'Can a man hide himself in secret places so that I cannot see him? declares the Lord. Do I not fill heaven and earth? declares the Lord." There is nothing you've done the Lord didn't already plan for. So, if He knows us, then why don't we trust in Him? We should; the Proverbs writer tells us (in Proverbs 3:5-6) to "Trust in the Lord with all thine heart"! This verse didn't say 80 percent of the time or only on Sundays. It says fully trust in God. Then it goes on to make us a promise, "Lean not unto thy own understanding. In all thy ways acknowledge him, and he shall direct thy paths." Another version (GNT) says, "Never rely on what you think you know."

Here's a revelation I'm going to share with you: you're not that smart, and you're not that good. You need guidance from the problem solver; not just any but the problem solver. The Holy Spirit is our guide, and we should rely on Him at all times: in our daily life, our eating habits, our hangouts. God needs to be intertwined in everything we do.

Then the verse goes on to say that after you have acknowledged Him, "He shall direct thy paths," meaning that He will give you direction, and when God makes a promise, He fulfills His Word. This should be a motto we live by. Don't know how you're going to pay your bills this month? Trust God! Don't know how you're going to beat cancer? Trust God! If something seems that you can't do it, or something's out of your control, that means it's time to trust God. He is the author and finisher of our faith.

As we continue down this path, continue to trust God when all the odds are against you. Trust God! It should be second nature to put your trust in Him. Trust Him and be thankful for what He is doing and has done in your life. Victory is the Lord's, and since you are His child, you are entitled to the benefits.

DAY 10

SCRIPTURES

"Consider it pure joy, my brothers, when you encounter trials of many kinds, because you know that the testing of your faith develops perseverance. Allow perseverance to finish its work, so that you may be mature and complete, not lacking anything."

— James 1:2-4 (BSB)

There are going to be times in these thirty days that you feel like you are a failure. Times you feel like you're not getting anywhere. This is the time to start pressing through; this is where you decide if you really want it. When you pray for something and persist for so long, there will be trials that try to take you out of focus. You have come this far, so don't give up. Yes, you may have stumbled or even contemplated giving up, but you will make it through, and after you finish this, you will make it.

When Moses was trying to convince Pharaoh, it seemed probably insane to keep showing up after those signs appeared. I mean, I would probably just stand there like, "Really, Pharaoh? You're going to act like you didn't see the water turn to blood and a zillion flies come out of nowhere?" This is funny now, but I can assure you it wasn't funny then.

Our trials can be a lot like Pharaoh's; they can be stubborn and hard to move. So, this means we have to be even more resilient to fight the old you from peaking its head around the corner. What's your purpose? Remember, the life you are currently living is not desirable. Sometimes we get foggy and lose our edge. Especially if you have a big goal, like losing weight or starting a new business venture. These are both mental, and you have to continue to fight through them no matter what.

DAY 11

SCRIPTURES

"Behold ye among the heathen, and regard, and wonder marvelously: for I will work a work in your days, which ye will not believe, though it be told you."

— Habakkuk 1:5 (KJV)

When fighting battles, or when things occur in your life (and trust me, they will occur), you can't be moved by them. Even when the storms around you seem to be thundering and rattling, you have to stand on the promises of God. The Bible says when you are right with God, even your enemies will be at peace with you (Proverbs 16:7). We know that God has never lost a battle and never will. Everything God has done was finished with Jesus. We have to know this one thing: God knew before we were conceived what kind of help we needed and what kind of guidance we needed. When problems arise, praise God even more.

Habakkuk the prophet was crying and praying for God to give him deliverance. He had sought direction from God, and he felt as if God didn't hear him.

It's funny how we go through things, and God shows Himself strong. Then time passes by, and something happens again, and we act as if He never shows up. He continues to do things over and over, and yet we question Him as if He has ever let us down. When was the last time He let you down? I can't think of one. God orchestrates our lives outside of our dimension. He doesn't need to send a receipt when He has gotten things in order.

When Habakkuk cried to God, the Lord told him, "Look at the nations and watch—and be utterly amazed. For I am going to do something in your days that you would not believe, even if you were told."

So, let's be clear, even if you heard what I'm doing, you would not believe me. God is not a fast-food restaurant; He doesn't deliver and do things on our time. We get so impatient with God, and we should be patient because what He is doing is far greater than what we could even imagine. So, stay steadfast and know that God is moving on our behalf.

DAY 12

SCRIPTURES

"To know wisdom and discipline, to comprehend the words of insight, o receive instruction in wise living, in righteousness, justice, and equity, to impart prudence to the simple, knowledge and discretion to the young—let the wise listen and gain instruction..."

— Proverbs 1:2-5

When I graduated from high school, my father and stepmother at the time sent us on a trip to Disney World. My stepmother was a CPA, and the company paid for our family vacation as kind of bonus. They went all out with this trip, we stayed in the Grand Floridian. It's Disney World's top-notch hotel... talk about favor. This place looked like something in a fairytale. It had tall white walls. Fountains and birds in the foyer, with a piano player in an all-white tux. Something truly mind-blowing.

When you go to a five-star hotel, there is a certain quality that is expected. They operate at another level which happens so effortlessly it slips your mind. The attention to detail at a hotel like this is so profound but yet so simple. They just do the little things right over and over again. The level of care they have for you at your stay is second to none.

How did this hotel get to this level? How did they incorporate these elements that have stuck in my head throughout the years?

The answer is wisdom. The only way for you to continue to grow and move forward is wisdom.

The devil wants us to be arrogant and stagnant, moving along in life with no purpose and vision. When you have wisdom, you begin to plan, and you show the Lord that He can trust you with more. How do you grow your brand? With wisdom. You need to understand your market, you need to know what's needed in your own company. Wisdom is the key. If you have wisdom, you can move along at a rapid pace. Wisdom is an accelerant; it can take you to new levels faster than talent and skill.

How do you get wisdom? Ask God for wisdom. He gives to His children freely. You are entitled to this.

Stay in prayer and stay grounded in this journey for the life you prayed for. You have a little over two weeks left. A lot can happen. Trust me, if you knew what God was doing right now, you wouldn't even believe it. *Hallelujah!*

DAY 13

SCRIPTURES

"Put on the whole armor of God, that ye may be able to stand against the wiles of the devil. For we wrestle not against flesh and blood, but against principalities, against powers, against the rulers of the darkness of this world, against spiritual wickedness in high places. Wherefore take unto you the whole armor of God, that ye may be able to withstand in the evil day, and having done all, to stand."

— Ephesians 6:11-13 (KJV)

Your goals should derive from the Word of God. They should have purpose and not be self-centered. Your goals should improve the kingdom of God.

I'm assuming you have had goals and a vision in the past you wanted to come to fruition. Maybe you accomplished 50 percent of them or 10 percent, or none at all. There is a reason you have not finished, and it is more common than you would imagine. We have so many variables as to why we don't finish things. Some would call these variables excuses. No matter how you twist it, if you set a goal and didn't follow through, then you made an excuse to quit.

Accepting your denial is huge in this phase because it shows growth, so go ahead and say, "It's my fault that I didn't accomplish my goals." Good job—you have successfully taken a huge step in becoming the person you wanted to be and who God desired you to be.

Now, here's another aspect to this. You are ignorant of the warfare going on around you. "For we wrestle not against flesh and blood, but against principalities, against powers, against the rulers of the darkness of this world, against spiritual wickedness in high places." The verse before says, "put on the full armor of God, so that you will be able to stand firm against the schemes of the devil."

Now, what schemes would the devil have against little old you? Why are you important to the devil and his forces? If he can knock you off and keep you sick, poor, out of shape, then he can keep you incapacitated. You have no testimony because you never pass the test. The best thing you can do for the devil is to stay stagnant. If he can keep you in the same place year after year, then he has won. It takes no faith to stay stagnant, and we know that it is impossible to please God without faith.

So why is it important for us to dream and set goals? Because it exercises our faith. It puts our faith to work, and this is how God moves in our lives. It's a chain reaction. If you accomplish your goals and you get everything you prayed for, then you are automatically a walking billboard for faith. Your life is a testimony, and it will give you the opportunity to say, "because of Jesus I was able to get here." If it wasn't for the blood, I wouldn't have His strength and His mercy to get me here. I am a new creature in Christ, and the old me is dead and gone.

Use this as motivation to inspire the next person. Let's finish our race and accomplish our goals to get the life we prayed for.

DAY 14

SCRIPTURES

"For God gave us a spirit not of fear but of power and love and self-control."

— 2 Timothy 1:7 (ESV)

"But I say, walk by the Spirit, and you will not gratify the desires of the flesh. For the desires of the flesh are against the Spirit, and the desires of the Spirit are against the flesh, for these are opposed to each other, to keep you from doing the things you want to do."

— Galatians 5:16-17 (ESV)

Two weeks down and a lifetime to go! We are building a foundation right now, and we are crushing it, I hope. If you are not giving this your all, then you need to take a step back and reevaluate what's holding you back. This is as mental as it is spiritual.

Today I looked back in my photos on my phone, and I went back as late as three years. I saw multiple times where I took a "before" picture of the body in regard to losing weight but never an "after" picture. This was very revealing to me and even disturbing. I reflected back as to why I never saw this drastic change. I'm sure at the time I took the pictures, I was as determined as ever. I mean, who takes a before picture without wanting to see major results. I've always been goal-driven, and I'm the guy who really dreams. I write huge and out-of-this-world dreams. I'm not afraid to say I'll move a mountain. So why was it that I didn't see this amazing after picture that was supposed to be so life-altering?

I pondered on what happened in my life that caused me to stop my journey. I came to one conclusion: discipline. I compartmentalized my discipline. I put priority over one goal more than the other when, in reality, they are all equal. I'm sure you're thinking, No way. I'd much rather make a million dollars, if this is your goal, than lose weight. So how are these goals the same? They are the same for one simple reason: you said you would accomplish them all. My grandfather used to tell me all the time, "If you say you are going to do something, you better be caught doing it and finish what you started." So, as I stated, I grew up on these morals, but I put emphasis on one thing versus another when they are all equally important. If I felt at that time that goal was important, then it doesn't matter how I feel a month later.

This brings me to my next conclusion: you can't be moved by emotions. We have been blessed by God to have emotions. They reflect Him. God has every emotion that we have, and I'm sure even more. Second Timothy says, "For God gave us a spirit not of fear but of power and love and self-control." So, God is telling us, "I didn't give you fear. Fear is a tool of the enemy because fear cancels faith." So how do we exercise fear if God didn't give it to us? Fear is the absence of faith; fear is the byproduct of our flesh being in control. When we operate outside of these emotions God has given us, they are derivates of Satan.

So, as we come to the end of fourteen days (two weeks), let's have those after pictures. Let's hit our PR (personal record) in business or in the gym. Let's read those three books a month. Let's build a gratifying life that is inspired by the Word of God and the Holy Spirit!

Keep going, you can do this!

DAY 15

SCRIPTURES

"More than that, we rejoice in our sufferings, knowing that suffering produces endurance, and endurance produces character, and character produces hope..."

— Romans 5:3-4 (ESV)

"Do you not know that in a race all the runners run, but only one receives the prize? So run that you may obtain it. Every athlete exercises self-control in all things."

— 1 Corinthians 9:24-25 (ESV)

Dave Ramsey said, "When the *pain* of '*same*' exceeds the *pain* of 'change,' you are ready to do what it takes to win." I want you to say, "Push!" Whatever you are going through, I want you to push through and continue this fight. We have to know it's going to get better; we have proof. I want you to instill this into your mental mind. You can accomplish anything you put your mind to.

I'm sure the last few weeks have been filled with trials. You maybe have felt like you haven't accomplished what you wanted. So, we must push. We are in this for the long haul. Confess it every day. "I will prevail. I will succeed."

There is something special that happens when you push past your limits. You can go to new levels. There is always more you can do, even when you think you have hit a wall. I want you to press through. When we press in, we create a new standard, a new way of thinking.

I remember training for football, and we would run gassers across the field. The coach would give us a time to finish them in, say, ten seconds. If anyone didn't finish in the appointed time, then he would add time. So this encouraged everyone to give their all for the duration of training. We would initially start off with maybe eight gassers. I always had to use the restroom before sprints. I think maybe my body was trying to get out of running. It never worked.

In the beginning, the first few gassers were relatively easy, but as we progressed, they quickly became a hassle to beat that time. We would have a few bigger guys who always fell behind getting yelled at, and the coach would give them time that suited their ability. As for everyone else, there was no excuse. By the seventh gasser, I was ready to pass out. I would see a bright white light, and I gasped for air like I was an asthmatic. By the time we finished the last one, I was ready to throw up, but I didn't. I figured if everyone else just did this workout, I should do more. So, I ran extra. I would continue to push my body. I knew that I was at my physical limit. My legs felt heavy, my chest hurt from breathing so heavy. I was literally drained. You would think that enough is enough. So, where did this extra strength come from to run additional gassers or stadium steps? This comes from pure willpower.

I remember some of my teammates would ask, "Are you in trouble?" or "Why are you doing extra? Are you trying to get brownie points (meaning I was trying to please the coach)?" Their comments were somewhat demeaning, but as time goes on, those were the guys watching me from the sidelines. I began to crush everyone in training and still have some left over to work harder. I tuned my body to go past its normal limits. If I had listened to my body, I would have been in the same place. The pain of staying the same outweighed the pain of change. I figured that overtraining would push me closer to accomplishing my goal.

This thought process created the lifestyle I live now. It carries over to the rest of your life. What you do in the midst of adversities matters. You have to know what you're working for. Once you realize this, it will have purpose behind the madness, and that madness will resolute in your life change.

DAY 16

SCRIPTURES

"For God so loved the world that he gave his one and only Son, that whoever believes in him shall not perish but have eternal life."

— John 3:16 (NIV)

Love is patient and kind; love does not envy or boast; it is not arrogant or rude. It does not insist on its own way; it is not irritable or resentful; it does not rejoice at wrongdoing but rejoices with the truth. Love bears all things, believes all things, hopes all things, endures all things.

— 1 Corinthians 13:4-7 (ESV)

Love is the most powerful thing in the world. It moves us in ways that no other emotion can. It can give us superhuman strength to save a loved one. It can give us the drive to move mountains. It can create masterpieces, art, music, movies. This is why God created us: to love. Love can cure illness; it can release hurt; it can create a new image, a new identity. Yet, we overlook it so much. We move around in this world with little to no knowledge of what love really is.

I always ask my friends, "Can a man who doesn't love God truly love a woman?"

I know this is a touchy subject, as some would say, "What about the atheist? Do they really not fall in love? Or the Muslim, do they never know love?"

I would simply say, "No! How could they? They have a counterfeit version."

If God is the creator of love, and in fact He is love, how could you know love if you never saw the original? How could someone who never saw the first duplicate the Mona Lisa? How could you cook your mom's famous cake without ever watching her? You can't because you have never been involved with the process; God's love for us is so deep and pure we can even fathom what love fully entails. So, once we draw closer to Him and we begin to take the focus away from ourselves, we begin to see the world through His eyes. We see the hurt, the agony His children are facing. We see the rim of why He gave Jesus to us. He loved us and knew that He would have to destroy His creation, a piece of himself. So, He had to come up with a contingency plan. That plan was Jesus. He was the reason. He was the point of it all. Isn't that so majestic? He truly is mind-boggling.

So, this love we need should be the fuel that drives us. This love should give us the strength to fight. Fight for the life that will influence the next person, and they will influence the next. This is how generational curses are broken. This is how generational wealth is established the right way. If you grow closer to Christ and strive to be better, you then are one step closer to your future self.

Ladies and gentlemen, I urge you to fight. I urge you, buckle up your pants and tie your shoes real tight because you are the difference-maker the world has been longing for. You are the spark that will change your world, that will eventually change the world. We can change the world, and we will. Amen.

DAY 17

SCRIPTURES

"You are the light of the world. A town built on a hill cannot be hidden. Neither do people light a lamp and put it under a bowl. Instead, they put it on its stand, and it gives light to everyone in the house. In the same way, let your light shine before others, that they may see your good deeds and glorify your Father in heaven."

— Matthew 5:14-16 (NIV)

Here's another way to put it: You're here to be light, bringing out the God-colors in the world. God is not a secret to be kept. We're going public with this, as public as a city on a hill.

On this day, we are going to take the focus off of ourselves and speak life into someone else. We have invested quite a lot into ourselves, and let's deposit some of that into someone else. We are starting to get the hang of things, and it's making sense. I'm sure if you are like me, the first three weeks have been strenuous, to say the least. So, making it to this point has been a miracle. I'm actually chuckling because I almost quit thirty times in seventeen days. We made it here, and we are ultimately different than we were a few weeks ago.

In all honesty, it feels good knowing that I'm pushing in a new direction. It's very challenging but at the same time amazing. I really have depended on the Lord the entire time, and each and every day, He has shown me himself. The things I've prayed for are becoming more visible. I can almost taste the fruition.

So now, let's push someone else to get where we are. Let's help another person, whether we talk to them or pray for them. I want you to think of one person that you feel God is leading you to. Write their name down and begin to speak life over them. When we put others in our crosshairs and begin to intercede on their behalf, we lose touch of our own struggles. We are the light in the world; the Bible even states we are the light as Matthew 5:14-16 (NIV) says:

> "You are the light of the world. A town built on a hill cannot be hidden. Neither do people light a lamp and put it under a bowl. Instead, they put it on its stand, and it gives light to everyone in the house. In the same way, let your light shine before others, that they may see your good deeds and glorify your Father in heaven."

Hallelujah, you are victorious through Christ. Your life is supposed to be a light for others. That means every facet of your life is to be an example.

DAY 18

Cleaning up is like cleaning the house. You don't say I'm going to clean up and move around with no plan. That will take you forever, and you might miss some things.

This is true with cleaning up your life. Yes, you speak, "I'm clean," but you have to identify what you're clean from. What is some catalyst that caused that uncleanliness? What are some areas that you need to focus on?

We are clean because Christ cleaned us first, then we were set free. Whom the Son sets free is free indeed. We are free from bondage; we are free from immorality. We are set apart and uplifted once we are set free.

Our lives are supposed to be judged. In fact, you should want it. Your life is the biggest witness you have. People should see the change. They should see how far you've come. It's not every day you see a total 180-degree change in someone. This is our pulpit; our life is our walking testimony.

When I create advertising campaigns, I often try and find that one thing to stand out in the ad so the message comes across clearly and effectively. The last thing you want as an advertiser is for someone to see your ad and not remember what they saw. The same should go for us. It should be obvious that we are new creatures. People should leave us and say, "They really have changed!" in awe, not in pity.

When Jesus rose from the dead, He was in His glorified body. This was obvious, He wasn't the same person who died three days prior. He had proof through the holes in His hands and feet. The witnesses were in awe that this was truly the Son of God! He gave directions and showed confidence that His life's purpose was fulfilled. We have this same power; we should walk with purpose Christ has won this battle and every battle we are going to face.

This is the Gospel; in Jesus, we have victory!

DAY 19

SCRIPTURES

"For as he thinketh in his heart, so is he: Eat and
drink, saith he to thee; but his heart is not with thee."

— Proverbs 23:7 (KJV)

What we call our self, matters; how we perceive our self, matters.

You see, in the Bible, what they named the child was important, and it typically was important in their life. We see names are
important all through the Bible. Jesus called himself Emmanuel.
We even see God rename Saul to Paul to rid himself of his past. So
this goes back to our confession and affirmations that we use over
our life. We are to be conscious of the words we speak of ourselves
and others. Choose life and not death; choose to create and not
destroy.

When I was in high school, my coach instilled in us to do right.
We would chant, "Do what? Do right! Do what? Do right!" This
was encouraging us to do the right thing at all times. We tend to
overlook small things and figure they don't mean much, but, in
reality, they mean so much. So, take control over your mouth and
your thought life. When things begin to look too hard or the old
you rises up, speak against it. When your life challenges rise us,
speak against them, remember you have authority over anything
with no soul, over objects and places...we are in control. Know
who you are and *whose* you are, in the name of Jesus.

DAY 20

Bring the kingdom glory, bring your family glory, bring your neighbor's glory. It should be a blessing to be around you. Wherever you go, people should see God's glory and favor over your life. We are His workmanship, His prize, and joy. So we should never be a burden wherever we go. The devil may try and rise up against you and convince you to sin or to fall back into your old lifestyle.

What does the Bible say about this? John 16:33 (ESV) says, "I have said these things to you, that in me you may have peace. In the world, you will have tribulation. But take heart; I have overcome the world."

Jesus is showing us we will have tribulation, so what is tribulation? Some of its synonyms are trouble, worry, anxiety, burden, cross to bear, affliction, ordeal, trial, adversity, hardship, tragedy, trauma, reverse, setback, blow, difficulty, problem, issue, misfortune, bad luck, stroke of bad luck, ill fortune, mishap, and misadventure.

We see the Bible doesn't say that once we are saved, everything will be peaches and cream. It clearly tells us that things will come to us, even things we can't control. But we do have power over them, and we do have dominion over evil. God does not allow us to keep that same mindset we once had once we are saved.

There also comes a time where God will remove certain people out of your life; where you are going, they can't go. They must be left behind in order for you to advance, especially if they're not sold out for God. Now, do we treat them like strangers? No, we still love them the way Christ intended for us to. We just have to know our new path doesn't include them, and we have run our course.

So, you have to be ready for this new lifestyle if you trust God. He will take you to new heights; He will place people in your life that are to take you higher and go to the next level. Take your hands off the reigns and let God be the coach. He will never leave you or forsake you.

DAY 21

SCRIPTURES

"The name of the LORD is a strong tower: the righteous runneth into it and is safe."

— Proverbs 18:10 (KJV)

We are three weeks in, and there should be some things you can look back and be proud of. I know that my goals have been tough, but I have persevered. It's amazing what can happen when you take your goals one day at a time. We will press in and continue to push ourselves.

I want you to create the life you want in your head. Where do you see yourself in the future? What do you look like, what type of clothes are you wearing? What type of home do you own? What have you accomplished? What are you doing that will contribute to this vision? I need you to replay this vision in your head over and over, and when doubt comes in your head, you visualize the end. Put your scriptures in place and declare the vision you have set in place.

What do we need to get rid of? What is something that we can do that can put us one step closer to our destiny?

These are my thoughts for you today. Are there things that need to be adjusted in your life? I want you to be very detailed in this because we are closer than we have ever been for a change. We have fought with these things in our life for years, and we are eradicating them. Now is not the time to be distracted but to press in. Go to a new level, and see what God has in store for us. We have to prioritize purpose over passion, over pleasure. Because ultimately, our purpose will bring us those things at the right time. We just have to stay disciplined and rely on the strength of the Lord.

Proverbs 18 says, "The name of the LORD is a strong tower: the righteous runneth into it and is safe."

DAY 22

Being authentic to the Word of God is our goal. We want to be great stewards of what God is doing in our lives. God has a plan for each of us, and if you pay attention, you can trace the moments in your life that have altered it. You are so important to God that He numbered the hairs on your head.

So why don't we treat ourselves like we are important? Why do we constantly try and figure things out without acknowledging God first? He is the best problem solver, the best advice giver. He is all that we need.

In His kingdom, we are heirs to the throne. The Bible even says that we are joint-heirs with Jesus Christ Himself. As an heir to the throne, you are entitled to so much. A king's kid can go anywhere in the kingdom, and the citizens of that kingdom acknowledge him or her as they would the king. There are consequences for mistreating a child of the king on earth, so what do you think would happen if we walked in this same revelation with God?

I love watching medieval times movies. The way of life then was very harsh and sometimes brutal. They have such a respect for the hierarchy... as they should. The king eats at a massive table with tons of food and servants. He always has party guests.

DAY 23

SCRIPTURES

"Therefore I say unto you, Take no thought for your life, what ye shall eat, or what ye shall drink; nor yet for your body, what ye shall put on. Is not the life more than meat, and the body than raiment?

Behold the fowls of the air: for they sow not, neither do they reap, nor gather into barns; yet your heavenly Father feedeth them. Are ye not much better than they? Which of you by taking thought can add one cubit unto his stature? And why take ye thought for raiment?

Consider the lilies of the field, how they grow; they toil not, neither do they spin: And yet I say unto you, That even Solomon in all his glory was not arrayed like one of these. Wherefore, if God so clothe the grass of the field, which to day is, and to morrow is cast into the oven, shall he not much more clothe you, O ye of little faith?

Therefore take no thought, saying, What shall we eat? or, What shall we drink? or, Wherewithal shall we be clothed? (For after all these things do the Gentiles seek:) for your heavenly Father knoweth that ye have need of all these things. But seek ye first the kingdom of God, and his righteousness; and all these things shall be added unto you."

— Matthew 6:25-33 (KJV)

Edward Venters

————————————

Do not worry!

DAY 24

Yesterday should have spoken volumes to you as to what I'm trying to impregnate into you. God is our provider in every area of our life.

When we were in the world, before Christ, our provider was our job, our resource was money, and they were our master to an extent.

When we get saved, this totally changes the narrative. Our Provider is God, and our resource is faith. Money becomes a tool and not a resource. We are in God's economy, and His blessings don't take credit cards; they take faith.

We see the natural every day, so we become consumed in the world's economy. We see price tags on homes and food, taxes and tariffs are entangled in everything we need and desire, but God says in chapter 6 of Matthew, verse 26 (KJV),

> "Behold the fowls of the air: for they sow not, neither do they reap, nor gather into barns; yet your heavenly Father feedeth them."

What is He saying here? The birds don't forward think anything. As a matter of fact, they don't even have a garden they own. But they eat and are taken care of. God is telling us that our everyday needs are nothing to Him. We need faith to access our wants. See, we don't need faith for God's promises; we just have to be aware of them. He even goes on to say in verse 31,

Edward Venters

"therefore take no thought, saying, What shall we eat? or, What shall we drink? or, Wherewithal shall we be clothed?"

Hallelujah, He says don't even think about it. That should be the furthest thing from our minds. We just have to stay grounded in His Word.

The bottom line is we have to quit putting God in a box. You can't contain God or His blessings. The problem is we try and calculate how God is going to bless us. This causes us to assume, which can lead to false judgment on our behalf. We need to be leery of how we pray and even talk so that God can bless us.

We are His children, and everything we need is already taken care of.

DAY 25

Leadership is a common key to success. Even people who often possess great following skills still exemplify great leadership skills. Being a leader is always sought after but never a role everyone fully wants. There is great responsibility in being a leader.

What drives someone to be a leader? What makes others want to follow them? This is something that will always be a part of human beings. From birth, we have a leader that is usually our parents or guardians. We have teachers who lead us and TV heroes whom we treasure. There is always a leader in the mix.

We tend to be tied to people who possess the same characteristics as us or what we see in ourselves. We love the power and the strength one possesses. The underlying thing we truly stand in awe of is discipline. We admire people who sacrifice, people who put it all on the line. People who go all out, all the time. I know I sure do. Nothing inspires me more than seeing someone excel in their craft.

We see this time and time again in the Rocky movies. Rocky is the hero, but he always seems to be the underdog.

DAY 26

As we continue down this road, I want you to speak something into your life this week. I want you to claim it and stand by whatever it is you claim. Don't back down—stand firm on it, pray about it, and let God take control of the situation. We are going to put our faith into work here.

Don't be scared to speak it. The moment you allow fear into your head, it will cancel the vision. Yes, this is big. Yes, this is going to stretch you, but that's what this book is all about. The Bible says it is impossible to please God without faith. Meaning we can do all the rituals and traditions, but if we don't utilize faith, then everything is useless. We give God an opportunity to show up in our lives when we speak something.

So get ready for whatever God is going to do this week. Speak it, and stand on it. Once you speak it, leave it alone.

DAY 27

Love and sacrifice go hand in hand. You cannot love something and not sacrifice. Sacrifice is what validated your love for something. We see this form of sacrifice with parents and husbands and wives mostly. This love can also come from material things.

People will sacrifice anything for money, sometimes even morals and ethics. That's why the Bible says, "The love of money is the root of all evil." People misquote this scripture all the time. Money is not evil. It's the love for it that's evil.

Everything we love should edify God, even our leisure items. They should be a reflection of Christ.

DAY 28

Forgiveness is such a huge objective in our life. Some people walk around with so much hurt and pain in their life, and they hold it in until they burst. Usually, the burst is big, and sometimes it's life-altering. But the truth is, it has to come out.

Many times, we try and bottle things up, and we cope with drugs and alcohol. Sometimes hobbies like running or lifting weights cover our faults, but the true mission is to be self-sustaining. You should be happy no matter if you can access those vices or not.

I had an altercation with my family. One of my family members felt as though the other hadn't treated them fairly. We knew they were angry all the time, but we had no idea why they were angry until I just simply asked why. Sometimes we just have to listen to people and hear what's wrong with them. There's always more to the story than what meets the eye.

We are obligated as Christians to help our fellow brother or sister. Help them overcome their demons and help them heal. Healing is a byproduct of forgiveness when we aim to heal and heal others; this changes our life and our world.

DAY 29

You have to stay on your path and your truth, no matter who doesn't like it. You have to do what's best for you. When it seems like the world around you is burning down, you have to stay steadfast with the Word of God and what you have committed to. Never settle and never take anything less than what you have been praying for.

When we pray for something, we wait until God brings it to pass and expect what we prayed for. God will never fulfill a promise halfway. He will never kind of do what He says, so you shouldn't accept it until you know for a fact that's what God has for you. So many times, we pray for something, and then something similar to what we prayed for comes along. Similar as in, it's kind of like what we prayed for but not all the way. That means it's not what we prayed for then.

We have to know that God fulfills our promises, and He never says no when it's aligned with the Word of God.

DAY 30

SCRIPTURES

Now, the Lord's Spirit had left Saul, and an evil spirit from the Lord tormented him. Saul's officials told him, "An evil spirit from God is tormenting you. Your Majesty, why don't you command us to look for a man who can play the lyre well? When the evil spirit from God comes to you, he'll strum a tune, and you'll feel better." Saul told his officials, "Please find me a man who can play well and bring him to me."

One of the officials said, "I know one of Jesse's sons from Bethlehem who can play well. He's a courageous man and a warrior. He has a way with words, he is handsome, and the Lord is with him."

Saul sent messengers to Jesse to say, "Send me your son David, who is with the sheep."

Jesse took six bushels of bread, a full wineskin, and a young goat and sent them with his son David to Saul. David came to Saul and served him. Saul loved him very much and made David his armorbearer. Saul sent [this message] to Jesse, "Please let David stay with me because I have grown fond of him."

Whenever God's spirit came to Saul, David took the lyre and strummed a tune. Saul got relief [from his terror] and felt better, and the evil spirit left him.

— 1 Samuel 16:14-23 (GW)

Thirty days in; hallelujah! God is so good. We have made it a whole month on our journey. Are you where you expected? How do you feel? Write these answers down, and we will come back to them.

Let's talk about worship and how important it is for us to have our personal worship time with God. I personally enjoy worshiping in the car, especially on the highway. Sometimes I go forty-five minutes to an hour of just pure worship. I hear from God in these times, I release stress and anxiety in these moments, and I deal with the enemy as well. When we worship God, we lose every demonic attack that comes against us. This is even biblical; when Saul was the king, he summoned David to the kingdom to sing and play the harp. The Bible said that a heavy spirit was upon Saul, and when David began to worship, the spirit lifted from him.

Today was a family day; it's the week of my mom's birthday, and I decided to take her to Pappadeauxs. It's a locally owned seafood restaurant popularized by the southern folks. One of my favorite places to visit when I come to see my mom. We began to eat, and like any dinner, we had a light conversation. We talked about the day and our task that we had individually. This was special because we haven't seen each other in a while. Our family is important for one reason: fellowship. We would not have this conversation with a random person, but we took the time out to discuss even the most mundane task. Why? Because we care for each other, and each family member matters. Now we have this access to discuss because of one reason: our blood. Our blood gives us validation to love the other person differently than we would a total stranger. It gives you access to the innermost thoughts and sides of a person, even if you haven't seen them in years. This is even more true with Christ. We have access to God because of the Blood of Christ. This validates our relationship and gives us the access to use His power freely. We are family with the highest, and with that, we have several perks. Remember who you are and that you can talk to the Lord any day and anyway. Thank God for the blood!

As you continue to walk out your journey and continue to accomplish your goals, just know you are covered by the blood. Your goals and everything you ever needed were already approved by God. He has prepared a way for you. Use this as a tool to teach others, spread what you have learned in the last thirty days, and continue to prosper. You are a new creature in Christ, and the old creature has passed away. God bless!

9 781637 694626

TIMOTHY CARTWRIGHT

|TRUE|
|SYMBOLS OF|
|YESHUA'S|
|BIRTH|

Little Known Facts about the
Anticipation and Arrival of our Messiah

Trilogy Christian Publishers
A Wholly Owned Subsidiary of Trinity Broadcasting Network
2442 Michelle Drive
Tustin, CA 92780
Copyright © 2024 by Timothy Cartwright
Unless otherwise noted, scripture quotations are taken from the
New American Standard Bible® (NASB), Copyright © 1960, 1962,
1963, 1968, 1971, 1972, 1973, 1975, 1977, 1995 by The Lockman
Foundation. Used by permission. www.Lockman.org.

10 9 8 7 6 5 4 3 2 1
Library of Congress Cataloging-in-Publication Data is available.
ISBN 979-8-89333-065-3
ISBN (ebook) 979-8-89033-066-3

Dedication

This book is dedicated to my beautiful wife, Annette, and my four adult children, Ryan, Sarah, Colby, and Seth.

Foreword

When you thought there was nothing more you could learn after a lifetime of hearing "The Christmas Story," this book turns just about everything on its head. Tim is an avid researcher and passionate follower of Jesus (Yeshua), and this book is an outflow of that.

I know Tim's heart, have listened to his teaching on this subject, and have been deeply impacted following the journey to Migdal Eder. Not only will the next Christmas look different, but the perfect timing and positioning of the Father in sending His Son for each of us has the potential to change lives eternally.

I believe this book is part of a pioneering journey back in time that is gradually being discovered by those who will stand back and be prepared to put tradition and centuries of sincere, but often erroneous, teaching on the miraculous reincarnation of our Savior to one side and start again following detail by detail the plan of salvation.

Read this. Pass it on and stand in awe of a God Who set in place the details of Jesus/Yeshua's birth before the foundation of the world. May thousands discover the wonder of Migdal Eder and, like the angels say, "Glory to God in the highest."

Daphne Kirk
www.G2gMandate.org

Acknowledgments

This book was indeed a labor of love and required a lot of patience from everyone who helped with this project.

First, I want to recognize my wife, Annette, for her never-ending support for this book. She spent countless hours debating my stances and proofreading text. Her devotion and support were priceless in this endeavor.

Second, I want to praise the work of my friend, Taylor Morse, who spent hours designing the graphics for my company's logo. He is a talented artist and a great friend. Thank you, Taylor.

Next, I want to recognize Daphne Kirk for encouraging me to publish all my papers. Daphne, this is just the first! She, too, loves to debate topics from various angles, which helps me provide meaningful answers during presentations. Daphne wrote the fantastic Foreword for the book and is a special friend.

Fourth, I want to thank my sister, Jill McGuire, for her endless hours reading my reports and providing great feedback. She has an M. Ed. degree and is one of the top teachers in Tennessee. I am blessed to have such an excellent resource for keeping my compositions in order.

Finally, I want to recognize Katharine Van der Beek, my Israeli tour guide and friend, for her drive to dig deep into the facts about every site on her tour routes. She is as passionate about Migdal Eder as I am. Her techniques, tenacity, and presentation exemplify integrity and professionalism. I highly recommend Katharine as a guide for anyone planning to tour the Holy Land.

Table of Contents

I. Introduction

When I think back to my childhood days, I paid little attention to the deeper meanings of Christmas. Of course, my mother would read the Christmas story from Luke and emphasize that *Jesus was the reason for the season*. We would decorate the tree and participate in all the secular things about the holiday. But I never thought of or appreciated the 4,000 years of history, prophecies of the coming Messiah, or the validity of anything about Christmas I was celebrating. It was in my 40s that I began studying the origins of Christmas. As it is known in America, Christmas has little authenticity regarding the true meanings and actual events around Yeshua's (Jesus') birth.

Our family nativity scene always included a wooden shelter with the standard goats, sheep, and cattle, along with the shepherds and Holy Family. Infant Yeshua (Jesus) was lying in a wooden trough. There was never a thought of an alternative to this layout. However, about five years ago, I heard about Migdal Eder as the possible site of Yeshua's birth. It was so intriguing that I began to investigate this place immediately, an endeavor that has culminated in the writing of this book.

And why do we celebrate the 25th of December as the birth date? What the ancient writers had to say about birthdays surprised me. Josephus, p. 973, says the law does

11

not permit us to hold *festivals at the birth of our children.* Early church father Origen, p.1716, said this about birthdays, ...*the worthless man who loves things connected to birth keeps birthday festivals, but we...find in no scripture that a righteous man marked a birthday.* No wonder no one kept up with Yeshua's birth date. Early Christians and Jews didn't celebrate anyone's birthday because it was considered a pagan activity. As a result, December 25 is most likely dubious because of the different dates observed in ancient times. For example, Elesha Coffman, in Christianity Today, lists at least nine other dates that celebrated the birth in the first 300 years. The date of December 25 was the convergence of pagan rituals and the early church's identification with the celestial sun. *Western Christians first celebrated Christmas on December 25, 336, after Emperor Constantine had declared Christianity the empire's favored religion.*

An article by Leo Hohmann, in WND 2014, is based on the research of Rabbi Jonathan Cahn called *The Mishkan Clue,* which sets out to solve two mysteries – the time of Jesus' birth and why it matters. Very few scholars believe that December 25 is the actual birth date, and Cahn verifies the conclusion with his research. In the article, Cahn says December is probably the least likely time for a Jewish couple from Nazareth to be traveling to Bethlehem for the Roman census while the woman, *Mary, was pregnant. Not only would the weather be too cold and rainy that time of year for shepherds to be out in their fields as the gospels say, but the Romans would not have held their census during the winter...In the church record, it's hard to find a credible reference to Dec 25 as Christ's birth date before the 4ᵗʰ century time of Emperor Constantine. More than likely, this date was picked to line up with the Roman holiday of Saturnalia, which was celebrated with the pagan sacrifice to Saturn...followed by gift-giving and a carnival-like atmosphere.*

Another tradition that has nothing to do with the birth of the Savior is the use of the Christmas Tree. Chastagner and Benson, in *Plant Health Progress*, say the earliest uses of trees as part of a ritual was in the 7ᵗʰ century, for pagans worshiping the winter solstice. It wasn't until the 1600s that the Christmas celebration replaced the pagan ritual. Christmas trees were first used in America by the German Hessians who joined the British in the Revolutionary War. The Christmas tree in America wasn't widely used until the late 1880s.

This religious awakening didn't stop with Christmas. What about the cross? The Latin cross, as we know it today, first appeared in 334 AD on a coin minted by Constantine. Before this, my research showed that the Hebrew tav +, and the Samaritan monogram qoph-tav were popular in the centuries prior. However, these were originally Jewish symbols and were later re-purposed by the Romans to hide their Jewish history. The ancient Hebrew tav meant *promise or covenant*, while the qoph meant *head*. The qoph-tav monogram served as a visual image of a suffering

Messiah on a cross.

There were other things just as shocking – such as the name Jesus. Lasson, M., in GrammarHow.com, shares that the name spelled J-e-s-u-s wasn't used until the *J* was invented in the 1500s. I found that before this, His name was a difficult-to-pronounce transliteration of the Greek letters *ieu-sous*. Transliterations are not established words – only a mix of letters to closely resemble the sound of a target word. Later, a *definition* is pinned on a transliteration to make it *official*. As a result, throughout this book, He, Jesus, will be referred to as Yeshua except where quoted. It is the name that His mother gave Him through the instruction of the angel. In Hebrew, the name means salvation.

This book's purpose is to share my findings from the ten-plus years of research that led to an exciting set of authentic signs and symbols surrounding Yeshua's birth. There is convincing proof that certain ancient groups knew the dates of his birth and death within a few years. Precursors pointed to the coming birth of the Messiah, and righteous people were aware of the prophecies. Chapter 9 in the Book of Daniel is the prophecy that provided a very detailed timing of the Messiah's time on earth. The Jews had to watch for an official decree that gave them permission to rebuild Jerusalem and then count 483 years ahead to know when the Messiah would be crucified. Can this date range be refined further? I think so. Numbers 24:17 says...*I see him, but not now; I behold him, but not near.*

I. Introduction

A star will come forth from Jacob, and a scepter will arise from Israel. Early writings, like the Damascus Document, reveal the interpretation of this verse as meaning there will be two Messiahs: One will be a Davidic-like King and the other a Priestly leader from Aaron's lineage. Which one comes first? No one knows their thinking, but they probably prepared for both. This means that the Levite leader from the line of Aaron, during his lifetime, would have to follow the requirements found in Leviticus. A significant command is Leviticus 8: 25-26, stating that Levite Priest could only serve between the ages of 25 and 50. This can be used to narrow the date of birth between 20 BC and 5 AD. Please see Appendix 6 for the details of this calculation.

As time grew closer to His birth, Jews and Samaritans developed and displayed their unique symbols of the coming Messiah – these were the tav and qoph-tav mentioned earlier. Further, my research brought me to Judea's last king and high priest (Mattathias Antigonus), who partially fulfilled the Messianic prophecies, including flogging and crucifixion. The Magi, whose ancestors were trained by Daniel, diligently watched for a divine alignment in the given timeframe. Shimon (Simeon) and Channa (Anna) faithfully stayed in the temple praying and watching for the infant Yeshua to be brought in on the eighth day after His birth.

To sum it up, Yeshua's birth did not surprise those who had studied the scriptures! His birth was not hidden; it was not unknown. It was very much anticipated by those who were righteous, faithful to the Word, and knowledgeable of the prophecies. Yeshua's birth occurred exactly where Micah 4:8 prophesied it would be – at Migdal Eder, where priestly shepherds tended to the Temple flock and infant Yeshua was swaddled in a unique wrap. Micah 5:2 confirms the location as Bethlehem, *But you Bethlehem Ephrathah, who are small among the clans of Judah, out of you will come forth for Me one to be ruler over Israel. One whose origins are of old from the days of eternity.*

This was a big deal to the people of ancient Israel. Even Origen, p. 453, said the birthplace was quite popular and mentions tours in Migdal Eder as late as 200s AD.

II. Anticipation of the Messiah

A. Daniel's Prophecy

Chapter 9 in the Book of Daniel is the prophecy that Jewish and Samaritan populations worldwide were watching for their Messiah because of the timeframe in Daniel 9:24-27. These verses proclaim that the Messiah's ministry would end around 483 years after the decree to rebuild Jerusalem. Daniel 9:24-27 - *Seventy weeks have been decreed for your people and your holy city, to finish the transgression, to make an end of sin, to make atonement for iniquity, to bring in everlasting righteousness, to seal up vision and prophecy and to anoint the most holy place. So, you are to know and discern that from issuing a decree to restore and rebuild Jerusalem until Messiah the Prince, there will be seven weeks and sixty-two weeks; it will be built again, with plaza and moat, even in times of distress. Then, after the sixty-two weeks, the Messiah will be cut off and have nothing, and the people of the prince who is to come will destroy the city and the sanctuary. And its end will come with a flood; even to the end, there will be war; desolations are determined. And he will make a firm covenant with the many for one week, but in the middle of the week, he will put a stop to sacrifice and grain offering; and on the wing of abominations will come one who makes desolate, even until destruction, one that is decreed, is poured out on the one who makes desolate.*

There were three possible decrees related to the Temple and Jerusalem. The first comes from Cyrus in 537 BC, who allowed the Jews to return and rebuild the Temple. Second, Artaxerxes I, in 458 BC, gave the Jews permission to restore government and resume religious practices, and the third was issued by Artaxerxes I in 445 BC to rebuild Jerusalem. Here are the verses of each:

Cyrus 537 BC: Ezra 1:2-4 - *Thus says Cyrus king of Persia, The LORD, the God of heaven, has given me all the kingdoms of the earth and He has appointed me to build Him a house in Jerusalem, which is in Judah. Whoever there is among you of all His people, may his God be with him! Let him go up to Jerusalem in Judah and rebuild the house of the LORD, the God of Israel; He is the God who is in Jerusalem. Every survivor, at whatever place he may live, let the men of that place support him with silver and gold, with goods and cattle, together with a free-will offering for the house of God, which is in Jerusalem.*

Artaxerxes I 458 BC: Ezra 7:1-20 - *Now this is the copy of the decree which King Artaxerxes gave to Ezra the priest, the scribe, learned in the words of the commandments of the LORD and His statutes to Israel: Artaxerxes, king of kings, to Ezra the priest, the scribe of the law of the God of heaven, perfect peace. And now I have issued a decree that any of the people of Israel and their priests and the*

Levites in my kingdom who are willing to go to Jerusalem may go with you. Forasmuch as you are sent by the king and his seven counselors to inquire concerning Judah and Jerusalem according to the law of your God which is in your hand, and to bring the silver and gold, which the king and his counselors have freely offered to the God of Israel, whose dwelling is in Jerusalem, with all the silver and gold which you find in the whole province of Babylon, along with the freewill offering of the people and of the priests, who offered willingly for the house of their God which is in Jerusalem; with this money, therefore, you shall diligently buy bulls, rams, and lambs, with their grain offerings and their drink offerings and offer them on the altar of the house of your God which is in Jerusalem. Whatever seems good to you and your brothers to do with the rest of the silver and gold, you may do according to the will of your God. Also, the utensils given to you for the service of the house of your God deliver in full before the God of Jerusalem. The rest of the needs for the house of your God, for which you may have occasion to provide, provide for it from the royal treasury.

Artaxerxes I 445 BC: Nehemiah 2:5-8 - *I said to the king, If it please the king, and if your servant has found favor before you, send me to Judah, to the city of my fathers' tombs, that I may rebuild it. Then the king said to me, the queen sitting beside him, How long will your journey be, and when will you return? So, it pleased the king to send me, and I gave him a definite time. And I said to the king, If it please the king, let letters be given me for the governors of the provinces beyond the River, that they may allow me to pass through until I come to Judah, and a letter to Asaph the keeper of the king's forest, that he may give me timber to make beams for the gates of the fortress which is by the temple, for the wall of the city and for the house to which I will go. And the king granted them to me because the good hand of my God was on me.*

It is worth mentioning that there are debates in academia about successors, times of reigns, and names of kings during the fourth and fifth centuries BC in Persia. It isn't straightforward. But this should help. Artaxerxes I began his reign in 465 BC and fulfilled the second decree seven years later in 458 BC, as mentioned in Ezra 7. Twenty years into his reign was 445 BC, as mentioned in Nehemiah 2, when permission was given to rebuild Jerusalem. Eastman and Missler, pp. 138 – 141, in *Creator,* confirm the date of 445 BC after examining the kingly lineages and calculating the dates of Yeshua's birth. The Encyclopedia Britannica confirms that Artaxerxes I's reign began in 465 BC.

Of these three decrees, only the one from Artaxerxes I in 445 BC specifically directs the rebuilding of Jerusalem. So, let's look at the math to see when the Messiah will be crucified (be cut off).

First, the year 445 BC must be converted from a 365-day year to a 360-day year. Then, we can subtract that number from the 483 years.

365 x 445 = 162,425 days - then divide this by 360 - 162,425/360 = 451

483 – 451 (-1 for the zero year) = 30 – 31 AD as the time of Yeshua's death

Narrowing the date even closer involves the story of Mary and Elizabeth found in Luke 1:26-45. The angel Gabriel visits Mary to tell her she will become pregnant through the Holy Spirit and that her cousin Elizabeth is already six months into her pregnancy. Remember that Elizabeth's pregnancy with Yokanon (John) fulfills the prophecy in Malachi 4:5-6. I need first to address the confusion in this passage. Is John the Baptist Elijah? In Matthew 11:13-14, Yeshua says...*for all the prophets prophesied until John. And if you are willing to accept it, John himself is Elijah who was to come...* I take this in a spiritual sense and not a physical one.

Mary traveled to see Elizabeth. The baby inside Elizabeth leaped when Mary arrived. Elizabeth was filled with the Holy Spirit and proclaimed that Mary was blessed among women, and blessed was the fruit of her womb. At this point, Yeshua's birth is within a few months. How many people did they share this experience with? How fast did the story expand in the land?

Based on the anticipation of Simeon and Anna, found in Luke 2: 21-38, the news must have spread quickly. Simeon and Anna waited in the temple when Yeshua was brought there for His circumcision eight days after the birth. *...And there was a man in Jerusalem named Simeon; this man was righteous and devout, looking for the consolation of Israel; and the Holy Spirit was upon him. And it had been revealed to him by the Holy Spirit that he would not see death before he had seen the Lord's Christ. And he came in the Spirit into the temple. When the parents brought in the child Jesus to carry out for Him the custom of the Law, then he took Him into his arms and blessed God, and said, Now Lord, You are releasing Your bond-servant to depart in peace, According to Your word; For my eyes have seen Your salvation, Which You have prepared in the presence of all peoples, A light of revelation to the Gentiles, And the glory of Your people Israel.*

And there was a prophetess, Anna, the daughter of Phanuel, of the tribe of Asher. She was advanced in years and had lived with her husband seven years after her marriage, and then as a widow to the age of eighty-four. She never left the temple, serving night and day with fasting and prayers. At that very moment, she came up and began giving thanks to God and continued to speak of Him to all those looking for Jerusalem's redemption.

B. Samaritan Sign of the Messiah

The Samaritans were a branch of the Israelites who began to splinter from the mainstream soon after Moses received the Law in 1450 BC. They completely separated from the mainstream after David's sin between 1000 and 900 BC. The Samaritans were also diligently looking for the Messiah, but they knew Him as the *Taheb*, which means *restorer*.

In 1887, Professor Strack of the German Palestine Association asked for an interview with the Samaritan high priest Jacob ibn Harun. Professor Strack questioned him concerning the beliefs of his people. The high priest replied in a letter, saying that *their word Taheb refers to the prophet promised by the Lord...I will raise them a prophet... They interpret this as one who will teach the nations the excellent way and lead them to walk in it only so that the world will repent of its sin and become converted and purified from all evil.*

Fein, in *Samaritan Update*, says the Samaritans consisted mainly of three tribes – Ephraim, Manasseh, and Levi, and were part of the Northern Kingdom. They believed the Torah (plus the book of Joshua) were the only valid scriptures from God. Based on scripture, Mt. Gerizim was chosen as the location for their temple, and they set up a parallel system of worship and governing until they were taken into captivity around 722 BC. Only a tiny remnant of the original Samaritan population remained near Mt. Gerizim. It was from that remnant, hundreds of years later, that the woman at the well would have an encounter with Yeshua.

Unfortunately, the Samaritans may have only one

ancient rabbi with complete writings. His name is Marqah. His time on earth is intensely debated, but I believe he lived in the early first century. Most of his writings focused on Moses as the savior of Israel and on a coming Messiah. In Marqah, p. 186, the Messiah they sought was known as the Taheb. *The Taheb will come in peace to possess the places of the perfect ones and to manifest the truth. Give ear and hear! Abide in truth; purify your intents... For the Lord will judge his people, the people of the Lord, i.e. Jacob, a descendant himself and yet a chief root, and descendants from fathers to sons, right from Noah the origin to the Taheb his descendant. This statement brings to notice the perfect ones who were superior to all people. Therefore, he said, and have compassion on His servants. They will not be in poverty, nor will they be afflicted in judgment, for they walked in the way o' righteousness. They have a rest in the Day of Judgment from all retribution; their souls have relief within the kingdom. One will come in peace to bring in relief.... Furthermore, and have compassion on His servants... is a statement wholly glorious. The Taheb will arise and the Lord 'ill have compassion....*

Additionally, Yeshua is recorded in the Brit Hadasha (New Testament) as mentioning the Samaritans and even interacting with them. The most important encounter can be found in John 4:4-42 and is known as *the Woman at the Well.* Here is the story: *A Samaritan woman came to draw water. [Yeshua] said to her, Give me some water to drink. (For his disciples had gone off into the town to buy supplies.) So the Samaritan woman said to him, How can you – a Jew – ask me, a Samaritan woman, for water to drink? (For Jews had nothing in common with Samaritans.) [Yeshua] replied, Everyone who drinks some of this water will be thirsty again. But whoever drinks some of the water that I will give him will never be thirsty again, but the water that I will give him will become in him a fountain of water springing up to eternal life. The woman said to him, Sir, give me this water so I will not be thirsty or have to come here to draw water. ...The woman said to him, Sir, you are a prophet. Our fathers worshiped on this mountain, and you people say that the place where people must worship is in Jerusalem. ...The woman told him, I know that Messiah is coming; whenever he comes, he will tell us everything. [Yeshua] said to her, I, the one speaking to you, am he.*

The most telling statement in this passage is the woman's statement *I know that the Messiah is coming.* Marqah's teaching, combined with comments by the woman at the well, indicates that the Samaritans were anticipating the coming Messiah!

After studying numerous coins collected throughout the ancient world, I concluded that the qoph-tav monogram symbolized a suffering Taheb (Messiah) on the cross. The first use of this symbol was found on these coins from Armenia in 76 BC. The second coin was minted in Samaria and dated 4 BC with a prominent qoph-tav. My research shows that 11 ancient countries and regions used this symbol on coins in the first century BC.

How did the Samaritans know their qoph-tav symbol meant a suffering Messiah on a tree? The Samaritans would have been knowledgeable of Deuteronomy 21:22-23... *if a person has committed a sin carrying a sentence of death and he is put to death, and you hang him on a tree, his body is not to be left overnight on the tree, but you shall certainly bury him on the same day...* Combine this with Isaiah 53:5...*But He was pierced for our offenses, He was crushed for our wrongdoings; The punishment for our well-being was laid upon Him, and by His wounds we are healed.* Psalms 22:16...*For dogs have surrounded me; A band of evildoers has encompassed me; They pierced my hands and my feet.* Piece these verses together, and the qoph-tav monogram visually captures a suffering Messiah on a tree.

Hurtado, Artifacts, p. 135, picked up on the history of the qoph-tav monogram starting in the 200s AD. He used the Greek translation of the monogram – either tau-rho or staurogram. He calls it ...*The earliest virtual reference to*

26

*the crucified Jesus…*He was right about the meaning, but 300 years off on the earliest reference.

C. Jewish Sign of the Messiah

Beginning about 150 BC, Jerusalem temple scribes began placing the Hebrew tav in the margins of scrolls to indicate those verses related to the Messiah or the Last Days. The meaning of the letter tav is a sign, symbol, promise, or covenant.

One of the most spectacular finds of the Dead Sea Scrolls was an intact version of Isaiah dated to about 130 BC. The document was believed to be from a version written in 350 BC. An entire Isaiah scroll is on display in the Israeli Museum, and if inspected closely, you will find about ten small tavs (x or +) in the margins, marking verses that pertain to a coming Messiah and End Time events. Here are three verses associated with the tav in the margin translated by Professors Flint, P. and Ulrich, E. in association with the Israeli Museum:

> *Isaiah 49:7, Thus says my Lord, the LORD your Redeemer, Israel, and his Holy One, to one despised, to ones abhorred as a nation, to a servant of rulers-kings see and rise, and princes will bow down, because of the faithful LORD, the Holy One of Israel, the one who chose you…*
>
> *Isaiah 54:14, In righteousness you will be*

established; you will be far from tyranny, for you will not be afraid, and far from terror, for it will not come near you.

Isaiah 56:1, For thus says the LORD: Maintain justice, and do what is right, for soon my salvation will come, and soon my deliverance will be revealed.

D. Earliest Numismatic Uses of the Cross

It was after 150 BC that the *cross* began showing up on coins. First, they appeared on coins in the Diaspora, then on coins of the Hasmonean and Herodian dynasties. The dissemination of the *tav* as a *cross* on coins was widespread for a century or so. My collection revealed 19 countries, from Spain to India, that placed the symbol on their coins. Shown below is an example of the ancient tav on the coin. The first image on p. 29 shows a bronze coin from India around 150 BC, while the second is a bronze coin from Zephyrion, minted about 6 BC in southern Turkey.

One coin, however, deserves more explanation and is shown on the next page. It is a potin (lead alloy) coin from Celtic Gaul (Spain/France) dated to about 30 BC. It shows a crescent and star at the top, representing the Star from Jacob in Numbers 24:17. Below the crescent is a single tav representing God. Below the single tav is a wavy line that Meshorer p. 158 suggests is the boundary separating the Holy of Holies (or Heaven from Earth). Under the wavy line are two tavs representing the anticipated two Messiahs – a widely held belief at the time. Finally, a straight line across the bottom of the coin is held up by hatched lines – representing terra firma.

E. The Hasmoneans

According to the *Jewish Virtual Library*, in 167 BC, a Judean rebel group led by Mattathias the Priest and his son, Judah Maccabee, defeated the Seleucids and cleansed the temple in 164 BC. (This led to the celebration of Chanukah.) In 163 BC, the victorious Maccabees returned a sovereign nation that hadn't existed for centuries to the Jewish people. The meaning of the name Maccabees or Hasmoneans is unknown, but the name Maccabee is popularly known as *hammer*. The name Maccabee was eventually replaced by

Hasmonean around 135 BC. Soon after, successive rulers took both titles: king and high priest. This rejected the theology of two Messiahs, which was popular then, and plainly shows that one person could fulfill both roles. Each Hasmonean ruler proudly displayed the dual titles on their coins. A few coins depicted the tav, as seen below. John Hyrcanus, in about 135 BC, was the first to use the dual titles and was subsequently followed by Aristobalus, Janneaus, Salome, Hyrcanus II, Aristobalus II, and ended at the death of Mattathias Antigonus in 37 BC. The coin on the left is from John Hyrcanus and was minted around 106 BC, and the coin to the right was minted by Mattathias Antigonus in 38 BC.

F. Coins of Herod the Great

Surprisingly, the coins of Herod convey the anticipation of the Messiah within the remnant of dedicated Jewish religious believers. The main mint in Jerusalem produced small denomination bronzes that were crudely made – a hint that the Jews could have made these coins clandestinely without Herod's knowledge. The design of these coins was relatively simple, as nearly all reflected temple life in some fashion. A couple of variations of the diadem/table design are shown below. My conclusion for the movement of the tav into the diadem was a message to the population regarding the arrival of the Messiah. The coin on the left below was minted about 10 BC, and the arrow shows the location of the tav outside the open diadem, which means the Messiah hasn't arrived. The coin to the right was minted around 4 BC and illustrates the tav is now inside a closed diadem, meaning the Messiah has come.

There was a beautiful set of commemorative coins minted in Samaria dated year 3. The set was minted only one year and contains four denominations: a prutah, 2-prutot, 4-prutot, and 8-prutot. These coins have been fiercely debated over the date's origin and who they commemorated. The numismatic world staunchly supports the year 3 date as 37 BC to celebrate Herod's victory over Mattathias. After studying the designs and imagery on the coins, I came to a completely different conclusion. Although Herod's name is on the coins, the minted symbols portray religious overtones and meanings, and Herod was certainly not religious. Instead of the year 3 date meaning 37 BC, I believe that the year-3 date means the *third year after Yeshua's birth*, which lines up with 4 BC. Simply put, the Samaritans commemorated Yeshua's birth in 6 BC with a set of coins minted in 4 BC at the time of Herod's death. This makes me wonder if the Samaritans wanted to preserve Yeshua's birthdate because Herod died in late March, 4 BC. I have included an image of the 8-prutot coin below.

My conclusion of the meanings of these symbols includes 1) the Star of Bethlehem, 2) the royal victory of palm branches, 3) a ceremonial helmet of salvation, 4) a qoph-tav suffering Messiah, and 5) a ceremonial basin for the bride. Each of the other coins has different symbols but are just as meaningful.

III. Mattathias Antigonus – King and High Priest – And Messiah Precursor

From the time of Alexander the Great to a century after Yeshua's ministry, many candidates have claimed to be or been proclaimed as Messiah. The most prominent person of the group appears to be Mattathias Antigonus, who ruled Judaea for three-and-a-half years from 40 BC to 37 BC. Mattathias partially fulfilled some of the ancient prophecies, including scourging and crucifixion. Unknowingly, Mattathias laid the groundwork for the true Messiah's coming 30 years later. It is essential to know that Mattathias was not seeking the title of Messiah or Savior.

According to Norris, p. 534, Mattathias was born in 91 BC. He married his first wife, Rachel, in 66 BC. They had eight children before Rachel died in childbirth in 52 BC. Mattathias spent nearly his whole life dealing with troublesome family members and the politics of Judea and Rome. Finally, in 40 BC, he was installed as King and High Priest and immediately went to war with Rome and Herod. Despite this, Mattathias temporarily united the kingdom under a Godly rule.

The advent of the Maccabean revolt and the subsequent Hasmonaean dynasty appears to have re-evaluated the interpretation of Numbers 24:17. For the first time in Jewish history, leaders appeared to be taking responsibility for governmental and religious duties.

The coins minted during Mattathias Antigonus' reign from 40 BC to 37 BC proclaim him as High Priest in Hebrew and King in Greek. The following images show an 8-prutot coin from Mattathias:

The obverse shows two cornucopias with the paleo-Hebrew legend *Mattathias, the High Priest and Council of the Jews.* The reverse shows a wreath surrounded by the Greek inscription in capital letters, *BACILEWC ANTIGONOY*, interpreted as King Antigonus.

The Hasmonean Dynasty severely undermined the whole concept of a *two-messiah* theology and invited the possibility of one person fulfilling both roles as King and High Priest. This came true decades later in the Temple with the encounters of Simeon and Anna (Luke 2:25-38). Simeon proclaimed Yeshua as *Your salvation* and *the glory of Your people, Israel,* while Hanna spoke to all those around Him who were seeking *the redemption of Jerusalem.*

Connection Between Mattathias' Reign and Messianic Prophecy

Mattathias was the second son of King Aristobalus and fell out of favor with Rome. He attempted to seize power by force in 42 BC but was defeated by Herod. Not easily giving up his royal lineage to the throne, he joined forces with the Parthians fighting the Romans in Syria. So, beginning in 40 BC, with the approval of the Pharisees and controlling Parthians, Mattathias was proclaimed King of Judaea and High Priest. For his entire three-and-a-half year reign, he was in constant war against Herod and Rome. Mattathias slowly lost key territory to Herod and ultimately fought his last battle in the courtyard of the Temple, where he was captured in 37 BC.

Josephus records in Ant. book xvi, pp15 -16 a scene in the waning days of the war with Herod: *...Now the Jews that were enclosed within the walls of the city fought against Herod with great alacrity and zeal (for the whole nation was gathered together); they also gave out many prophecies about the temple, and many things agreeable to the people, as if God would deliver them out of the dangers they were in ...* The fact that Mattathias had gathered the nation to offer prayers and prophecy shows confidence that he was putting his faith in God.

The events after his capture also had some prophetical overtones. Herod paid large sums of silver and gold to Antony (of Cleopatra fame) to scourge and crucify Mattathias because Antony planned to take him back to Rome for victory parades. According to ancient historian Cassius Dio, book 49, paragraph 22: *...These people Antony entrusted to a certain Herod to govern; but Antigonus he bound to a cross and flogged, — a punishment no other king had suffered at the hands of the Romans...* Mattathias survived his crucifixion and was then taken to Antioch, where he was beheaded. Josephus, Ant. Book xv, paragraph 2, *... And Strabo of Cappadocia attests to what I have said when he thus speaks: Antony ordered Antigonus the Jew to be brought to Antioch, and there to be beheaded. And this Antony seems to me to have been the very first man who beheaded a king, as supposing he could no other way bend the minds of the Jews to receive Herod, whom he had made king in his stead...*

When exactly did all of this take place? Josephus, book xvi, paragraph 4, states,...*This destruction befell the city of Jerusalem when Marcus Agrippa and Caninius Gallus were consuls of Rome on the hundred eighty and fifth Olympiad, on the third month, on the solemnity of the fast, as if a periodical revolution of calamities had returned since that which befell the Jews under Pompey; for the Jews were taken by him on the same day, and this was after twenty-seven years.* There is much debate about which calendar and fast Josephus' was referring to for the third month. If he was referring to the Julian calendar, the third month is March, which lines up with Nisan, the time of Passover. The "Fast of the First Born" was celebrated in Nisan on the day before Passover. A second plausible fast is Tisha B'Av, the fast in the fifth month, meaning that the assault on Jerusalem began in the third month in the Hebrew calendar. It makes the most sense for Mattathias to be executed at Passover. Out of curiosity, I used my Stellarium astronomy program to search for heavenly formations around Passover that could be linked to Mattathias in 91 BC. It turns out that there was an impressive conjunction of five moving bodies at sunrise. Included were Saturn, Mars, Sun, Venus, and Mercury, which were tightly grouped. This alignment occurred at 6 a.m. on April 8, 91 BC. However, I do not know of any attempts, ancient or otherwise, to evaluate this formation. There is no way to confirm this, but this makes it plausible that Mattathias was born at Passover and died at Passover just as Yeshua did.

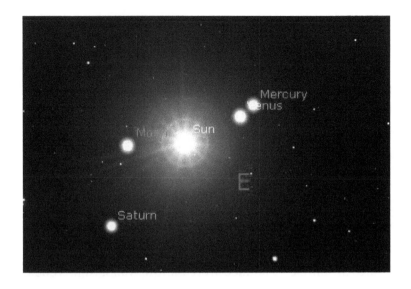

Of the many historical people who claimed to be or were proclaimed Messiah, Mattathias was the closest of them all. Many prophecies appeared to be fulfilled, but many more were not. What does it mean? Most likely, the entire reign of Mattathias seems to have been a precursor for preparing the Jewish population to receive their Messiah. Many events during his three and a half years as King and High Priest could be understood as fulfilling specific prophecies. However, the events involving Mattathias can't be considered total fulfillment – only as a preview of the Messiah to come 30 years after Mattathias's death.

This table shows the possible prophecies fulfilled by Mattathias Antigonus:

Possible Fulfillment	Mattathias' Action	Comments
Num 24:17	Born in 91 BC under a planetary alignment (Star)	Just after Pesach of that year, a spectacular conjunction appeared of the moon, sun, Jupiter, Venus, and Mercury at sunrise
Num 24:17 Ps 110:4	Ruled as both King and High Priest	Mattathias genealogy came from both David and Levi
Zech 9:9	Mattathias conquered the Romans and entered Jerusalem as King	There is no evidence that he rode on a donkey. Although it was common for new Kings to do so.
Zech 11:12	Money paid for his betrayal	Payment consisted of gold and silver. It wasn't specifically 30 pieces of silver.
Isa 53:5	Scourged and crucified	He survived his flogging and crucifixion, only to be beheaded.
Daniel 9:27	Rules 3 ½ years	Yeshua's first rule on earth was 3 ½ years. Mattathias's time wasn't preceded by a peace covenant but was followed by the sacking of the temple
Ps 16:10	Resurrected	Maybe he appeared dead but was only unconscious. Regardless, surviving a crucifixion is not resurrection.
Ex 12:46, Num 9:12	Messiah as Passover Lamb	Mattathias was scourged and crucified on Pesach but wasn't killed until weeks later.

Table #1   Partial Fulfillments by Mattathias

IV. Time of Yeshua's Birth

A. Star of Bethlehem

In *The Star of Bethlehem*, Dr. Molnar, p. 50, determined the meaning behind the *Ram and Star* coins from Antioch. Molnar's thorough research led to the most likely *heavenly alignment* that constituted the *Star of Bethlehem*. He concluded that the sign was meant to recognize the birth of the Messiah in Judaea on April 17, 6 BC. In 2014, an astronomer from Louisiana State University, Dr. Bradley Schaefer, presented a paper in Groningen, Netherlands, titled *Astrological and Historical Evaluation of Molnar's Solution.*

In it, Schaefer concluded: *Until the time of Kepler, the miracle answer was the default idea to explain the star... our conference in Groningen has been the popularization and a celebration of the new paradigm that has swept the field... Molnar's astrological solution is now the leading and default explanation for the star. So, with reasonable confidence, we now know that the Star of Bethlehem originated as a report of the natal horoscope for April 17, 6 BC.*

Dr. Molnar revealed compelling evidence on the Star of Bethlehem's source and the purpose of the star and ram design. He based his conclusions on the interpretation of scripture and ancient writings regarding astronomy by the Romans, Jews, Persians, and Greeks. The scene that sparked his research is shown below in the coin's reverse. This coin was minted in 6 AD in Antioch, later becoming one of early Christianity's centers. Ancient writings show that Aries the Ram represented Judea in the zodiac and revealed the particular positions of the other heavenly bodies that revealed regal divinity. In Molnar pp 67-69... *the sources for these astrological effects are the works of Ptolemy, Dorotheus, Valens, Firmicus, and other astrologers ...who referred specifically to several of these conditions in the horoscope of an emperor or king.* This is what the Magi would have known and caused them to go to Jerusalem.

Molnar, p. 98, found that an unusual array of the planets occurred in Aries during 6 BC – which the Magi recognized as a divine birth in Judea. This unique alignment is represented by the star next to the Ram's head. An essential fact from Dr. Molnar's work, p. 40, ...*astronomers [Magi] developed the mathematical means to predict positions of*

*the planets...their clever procedure was to match a set of observations made over a long period with a mathematical expression...the astronomers [Magi] used this to predict the skies for other dates...*in other words, the Magi meticulously tracked the position of all the bodies. They didn't necessarily have to view the particular alignment. This opens the possibility that the Magi anticipated the birth based on their calculations and began their trek to Jerusalem months earlier to coincide with Yeshua's arrival.

This makes more sense in Matthew 2:1-7, where the Magi appear in Jerusalem as they quickly find the infant Yeshua. Further, the fact that the Magi were in Jerusalem means they had to see the star in the east, which clarifies the second part of verse 2. If they had arrived much later, the Holy Family would have already returned to Nazareth, as reported in Luke 2:39, or Egypt, as reported in Matthew 2:13.

My first project on Stellarium was to verify Dr. Molnar's findings. It turns out that Dr. Molnar was spot on with his conclusions, and a screenshot of the morning of April 17, 6 BC, can be seen on page 47.

The incredible alignment of all seven heavenly bodies was exceptionally regal and divine. It was an event that only the Magi recognized. It began at sunrise, as Venus rose first while in Pisces. Venus was followed by Saturn, Moon, Jupiter, and the Sun, all in Aries. Finally, Mars and Mercury appeared above the horizon while in Taurus.

This was based on the complicated rules of the ancient astronomers mentioned earlier.

Until noon that day, all the planets kept their alignment except Jupiter, which passed behind the moon just after sunrise. This unique alignment is called the *Star of Bethlehem* and was meant for the Magi, not any other priest or politician. This is why Herod and the temple officials were surprised – they had not seen or interpreted any spectacular heavenly displays. Matthew 2: 1-7 says: *Now after Jesus was born in Bethlehem of Judea in the days of Herod the king, magi from the east arrived in Jerusalem, saying, where is He who has been born King of the Jews? For we saw His star in the east* [the heavenly procession] *and have come to worship Him." When Herod the King heard this, he was troubled, and all of Jerusalem with him. Gathering together all the chief priests and scribes of the people, he inquired of them where the Messiah was to be born. They said to him, "In Bethlehem of Judea; for this is what has been written by the prophet: AND YOU, BETHLEHEM, LAND OF JUDAH, ARE BY NO MEANS LEAST AMONG THE LEADERS OF JUDAH; FOR OUT OF YOU SHALL COME FORTH A RULER WHO WILL SHEPHERD MY PEOPLE ISRAEL. Then Herod secretly called the Magi and determined from them the exact time the star appeared.*

Here is the screenshot of my Stellarium program at sunrise on April 17, 6 BC, as it looked from Jerusalem:

As previously noted, according to the astronomy of the Parthians, what occurred on April 17, 6 BC was the most *Regal* or *Divine* set of signs possible, a unique heavenly event proclaiming the Messiah had arrived. Dr. Schaefer's estimate of the probability of this exact alignment is outside of every 12,000 years. Table #2 below lists the regal characteristics only the Magi would have recognized:

Saturn, Jupiter, and the Sun are all in Aries.
Moon begins its pass in front of Jupiter and completes the pass by the mid-heaven (noon)
Saturn and Jupiter are "spear-bearers" (rise before) for the Sun.
Mars and Mercury are "attendants" (rise behind) for the Moon
Venus is in Pisces

Table #2   Regal Signs of the Heavenly Arrangement

B. Why Aries?

Molnar, p 46, discusses the ancient references that relate Aries to Judaea. Ptolemy in *Tetrabiblos, Book II*, p, 46, says that *...Aries represents Coele Syria, Judaea,* *and Idumaea...* Vettius Valens, in *Anthology*, says that ... *Aries controls Palestine and adjacent lands...* Further, the Jewish Encyclopedia, section titled Zodiac, states ... *The twelve constellations represent the twelve tribes... The standards of the tribes corresponded to the zodiacal signs of the constellations, so that in the east was the standard of Judah, with Issachar and Zebulun beside it, these three being opposite Aries, Taurus and Gemini...* And even in modern times, *AstrologyWeekly.com* recognizes Aries as representing Israel.

Additionally, the Aramaic name for male lambs is *eem-rah,* which happens to be the Aramaic name of the constellation Aries (the Ram) that appears most prominently in the March to April time frame -- when the bulk of the lambing is taking place. The Jewish word for zodiac is *mazzalot,* and Nisan 1 begins the cycle with *eem-rah* being the first constellation in the spring. Outside of tracking the moon for God's chosen days (moedim), the Jews did not participate in astrology and wouldn't have recognized the regal heavenly alignment. From American Heritage Dictionary, ancient astrology...*was the art of judging the influences of the stars upon human affairs.*

C. Why the Magi?

The answer to this question requires an in-depth knowledge of the Book of Daniel. Daniel was an intellectual teenager taken into captivity by Nebuchadnezzar when

Jerusalem was sacked in 586 BC. The king recognized his intellect and abilities and he was specially trained to serve in the court of Nebuchadnezzar in Babylon. Through a series of dreams, interpretations, and miracles, Daniel became the king's favorite and rose to prominence within the kingdom. Daniel 2:48 says Nebuchadnezzar ...made him ruler over the whole province of Babylon and chief prefect over all the wise men of Babylon... Who are the *wise men* mentioned in this verse? Earlier in chapter 2, it is stated that the wise men comprised magicians, diviners, enchanters, sorcerers, and Chaldeans. The word Magi is short for *magician*. So, there is no mystery as to the wise men's origin described in Matthew's book. They were direct descendants of the very men trained, taught, and managed by Daniel some 500 years before the birth of Yeshua.

As mentioned earlier, the Messianic prophecies in Daniel chapter 9 are extremely helpful. Verses 24 – 26 provided a detailed prediction that the Messiah would arrive 483 years after a decree was issued to rebuild Jerusalem. The most likely date of the decree is 445 BC based on Nehemiah 2:5. When 483 years (360 day year) is considered and subtracted from 445, the date of the crucifixion ...when the Messiah is cut off... is around 30 AD. The Magi could narrow the time of birth to a minimal timeframe – probably within one year of Yeshua's birth.

This alignment was the culmination of a heavenly dance that began weeks before. According to Bedwell, in

Studies, Table of Holy Days, Nisan 1 fell on the equivalent of March 20 that year, and, most likely, Yeshua was born within that span between March 20 and April 17 in 6 BC. To the Magi, the alignment in the image on p. 47 was the absolute confirmation of the birth of the King of Israel.

Were there other heavenly alignments within a few years of this event? Yes, but nothing occurred that exceeded the majesty of the procession on April 17, 6 BC. In 7 BC-6 BC, there were four consecutive Saturn-Jupiter conjunctions in May, Sept, Dec, and Feb, but they weren't more spectacular than the alignment on April 17. Later, in 3 BC, there were some conjunctions that some claimed to be the *star* that didn't match the magnificence of the event on April 17, 6 BC alignment.

D. Lambing in Israel

I thought the time, or at least the season, of Yeshua's birth would be a straightforward exercise with wide acceptance. He was, after all, the "Perfect Lamb that was slain" -- so why wouldn't it be evident that he was born during the lambing season in Israel? It turns out that a significant movement is pushing the concept of an autumn birth tied to Sukkot. I had to dig deep for information about lambing in Israel at the time when the shepherds would be out all night with the flocks. The shepherds had two primary responsibilities: tending to birthing ewes and protecting the newborn lambs from blemish.

Back to Hohmann in the WND article, Cahn ruled out summer, autumn, and winter. This leaves only one option – spring. Cahn continues, *This would have been known as 'lambing' season in Israel. Only in the lambing season do shepherds watch their flocks by night...as described in the gospels. This would have been in late March and into April when shepherds were out watching for lambs to be born in the fields. Nisan 1 is the historical first day on the Hebraic calendar...it represents a new beginning.*

The most important source of information was the report by Professor H. Epstein, an expert in animal breeding at the Hebrew University in Jerusalem. Epstein, p. 2, begins with a history of the *Awassi sheep* that goes back 5000 years in Israel. The Awassi have been the primary breed of sheep in Israel, Syria, Jordan, Lebanon, Iraq, and Iran during that entire span.

So, for 5,000 years or more, the breeding season for the Awassi sheep has been between June and September. Research has shown that the ewes are not in estrus until the spring and summer when grazing has brought their body weight back to a level that could support pregnancy. Seventy percent of ewes give birth as a yearling. As a result, the bulk of lambing in Israel has been in March and April (the Hebrew month of Nisan) since the beginning.

Another point of contention is the swathing of the lambs at birth because this process was sparsely mentioned in ancient writings. A mundane event such as this didn't warrant documentation. However, God commands that all first-born males, including animals, are His (Exodus 13:12) and must be consecrated. Further, the commanded animal sacrifice procedure required the animal to be blemish-free. This means that the newborn male lambs had to be blemish-free firstborn males. These lambs would have been born at Migdal Eder, a focal point of this book, and will be discussed later.

Additional information from Epstein, p. 56, *During the lambing season, lambs born in the field ...too weak to follow their dams...are carried by the shepherds to the tents or villages where they remain for a few days until firm enough to join their dams at pasture...Such lambs are taken from their dams on the day of birth and fed milk from a small vessel. Their attachment to the shepherd takes place within the first ten days of life, the period of imprinting. Later, they are trained to eat grain from the hand of the shepherd.* This passage from Epstein supports the notion that the priestly shepherds took the newborn lambs back to Migdal Eder and, possibly, kept them there for up to ten days for the lamb to know the shepherd's voice. How well do we know our Shepherd's voice?

Epstein, p. 96, from Table 3-13, *a yearling is considered between 12 and 16 months old. In this study, there were no yearlings before January and no yearlings after June. Gestation is typically between 150 and 160 days.* The table in Epstein's document shows that *ninety-six percent of the sheep were born between February and May.*

Schoenian, *Sheep 201*, lists multiple hazards when lambing. Two of these are particularly important during birth. The first is hypothermia. The normal range for the body temperature of a lamb is 101 – 102 F, but on a cold night, when the lamb can't keep up with its mother, it can die from hypothermia when its body temperature reaches 98 F. The second condition involves the attention given to the wound of the umbilicus and possible bacterial infections if the lamb falls in the dirt.

From this, it is easy to conclude that the Levite shepherds had to be present at birth to inspect and protect newborn lambs. This was accomplished by swathing. But, this night, the infant Yeshua was wrapped in a unique garment, and the shepherds were directed by an angel, in Luke 2:12, as the way to find Him. What could this special wrapping be? Why didn't the angel direct them to look for His Parents and a midwife standing over Him? This seems like an odd request, but remember, on this night, it's possible that hundreds of swathed lambs, in the darkness of a new moon, were lying in and around Migdal Eder, and the wrapping had to be noticeable. Maybe this exercise was the first instruction to seek the Messiah diligently in a time of chaos!

I think the answer to the question about the wrap can be found in an Aramaic word in Luke 2:7. The key word in this verse is pronounced *krahk-ta-ha*, and it means not only wrapping but also *miter*. The definition of *miter* in multiple dictionaries is high priest's head wrap. This unique wrap was fine linen, known to be very expensive and exclusive to wealthy individuals and the treasury of the Temple. An assumption on my part is that after the angels appeared to the shepherds, one shepherd was sent to the temple to tell the High Priest of the visitation, who then supplied him with the wrap. Removing this gleaming white, unused part of the High Priest's headdress doesn't appear to have broken any rules. Please read Appendix 2 for more details about the headdress and Appendix 3 for more about linen.

E. Bethlehem

Here is the story we all know in Luke 2; the pertinent verses are shown. ...*While they were there, the days were completed for her to give birth. And she gave birth to her firstborn son, and she wrapped Him in cloths, and laid Him in a manger because there was no room for them in the inn. In the same region, some shepherds were staying out in the fields and keeping watch over their flock by night. And an angel of the Lord suddenly stood before them, and the glory of the Lord shone around them, and they were frightened. But the angel said to them, Do not be afraid; for behold, I bring you good news of great joy which will be for all the people; for today in the city of David, there has been born for you a Savior, who is Christ the Lord. This will be a sign for you: you will find a baby wrapped in cloths and lying in a manger. And suddenly there appeared with the angel a multitude of the heavenly host praising God and saying,*

Glory to God in the highest, and on earth peace among men with whom He is pleased. When the angels had gone away from them into heaven, the shepherds began saying to one another, Let us go straight to Bethlehem then, and see this thing that has happened which the Lord has made known to us. So they came in a hurry and found their way to Mary and Joseph and the baby as He lay in the manger. When they had seen this, they made known the statement which had been told them about this Child.

From Micah 5:2 *But as for you, Bethlehem Ephrathah, Too little to be among the clans of Judah, From you One will go forth for Me to be ruler in Israel. His goings forth are from long ago, From the days of eternity.*

The image above is from 2018 and was taken looking southeast to Bethlehem from the southernmost kibbutz in Jerusalem. It is a short distance from Jerusalem to Bethlehem to the south, and many think Midgal Eder was about halfway there. In this picture, the rugged valleys and hills are where the sacrificial lambs were raised and Yeshua was born.

The boundaries of the pastureland included the Hinnom Valley to the north, the Kidron Valley to the east, the town of Bethlehem to the south, and the ancient road from Bethlehem to Jerusalem to the west. All this area was considered Bethlehem. Bethlehem is situated roughly three miles to the south of Jerusalem, and it is approximately three miles to the Kidron Valley from the Bethlehem-Jerusalem Road. This makes the minimum area surveyed by Migdal Eder lookouts about nine square miles or 6,000 acres.

In Aramaic, from Oraham, p. 52 and in Hebrew, from *Do it in Hebrew* online dictionary, the town is pronounced bet – lechem. It is translated as House of Bread. Legend says it was where God taught Adam how to make bread. Bethlehem has been featured throughout history with significant events; see the table below:

Rachel died and is buried.
Ruth gleaned the fields.
Jesse (David's father) lived there.
David was a shepherd.
Samuel anointed David
Yeshua was born

Table #3 Important Events at Bethlehem

So, the *Bread of Life* was born in the *House of Bread*.

F. The Shepherds

The shepherds were not the Bedouins who are still raising sheep today; they were temple priests who had to ensure that the thousands of lambs were perfect with no blemish – that's why they were in the field all night long. They were watching for ewes giving birth to assist in the birthing and to keep the lamb from injury and blemish. They wrapped them in the swathing clothes and returned them to Migdol Eder for a few days.

Evidence that supports the claim they were Levitical priests comes from Edersheim, p. 186, who concludes that the shepherds were under *Rabbinism,* making them Levitical Priests.   From the Jewish perspective, the Mishnah Baba Kamma, 7.7 and 80a:11 say, *The Mishnah expressly forbids the keeping flocks throughout Israel... except in the wilderness...* (the only exception are those in Temple service...) and from Mishnah 7:4: *This mishnah deals with beasts (sheep, cattle, goats) found in proximity to Jerusalem. Since many animals around Jerusalem may have escaped sacrifices... we must treat them as if they were sacrifices. Beasts found in Jerusalem are from Migdal Eder and within the same distance in any direction...* (these excerpts can only mean that the priests were the shepherds.)

There is even a hidden meaning in the name Shepherd. From Oraham, p. 484, two words in Aramaic are used for shepherds: *reh-eh-ya* and *reh-eh-atah*. *Reh-eh-ya*h means "Sees God" and *reh-eh-atah* means "Sees You."

G. The Manger

By definition, a manger is a feed trough. In ancient times, the manger was carved out of local limestone, making it sturdy, reliable, and amazingly durable. Many can still be found lying about in Judea. The front cover of this book has an excellent depiction of a first century manger. However, some sources try to interchange manger with *booth, stall,* and *stable.* This nomenclature accompanies the Sukkot birth scenario discussed earlier. However, one manger became the crib to comfort our Lord and Savior on this night in first-century Judea. Migdal Eder guarded thousands of sheep in the Temple flock and would have required dozens of mangers to accommodate numerous births in the spring. It is not a stretch for the shepherds to have reserved a newly cut, unused manger for Yeshua after receiving the news from the angel. See Appendix 1 for more information on the Temple Flock.

Photo Credit: Jill McGuire, used with permission

In Dec 2022, my sister, Jill, toured the Holy Land and visited Shepherds Field, six miles southwest of Bethlehem. Most likely, it is not the location of Migdal Eder, but it does have authentic examples of mangers, caves, and ruins from the first century. There was a manger from Yeshua's time in a cave on site. The manger was severely damaged, with one-half of the stone missing. I guess that centuries of Pilgrams taking souvenirs took its toll on the manger. Her picture of the manger is shown above.

Jonathan Cahn discusses the theory about Yeshua's birth during Sukkot. The essence of the theory is that Yeshua was born in a sukkah and that this temporary shelter was later called a manger. *...while this is well-meaning and sounds nice, it would have been impossible for several reasons. First Jesus was born in a manger, and a manger is a type of feeding trough. Also, the spiritual meaning of the Feast of Tabernacles lines up with the end times and the closing of an era, not the opening or beginning of an era. Messiah's birth, death, resurrection, and second coming must come in the proper chronological order...*

But there is a much deeper meaning in the word *manger*. Oraham, p. 15, says the word for a manger in Aramaic is pronounced *aur-yah* or *or--yah*. The root word *or* means light, while *aur* means *lion*. *Yah* is an abbreviation for God.

So, when read in this manner, it means Yeshua, *the Light of the world*, was cradled in *the Light of God* as the *Lion of God.*

H. Migdal Eder

In Hebrew, Migdal Eder means *Tower of the Flock* and would have consisted of a top turret covered with limbs and leaves for protection from the weather and served as a lookout for predators and birthing ewes. Based on internet pictures, these towers could be as high as 20 or 30 feet. Migdal Eder had a cave underneath the tower for warmth, swathing, sleeping, feeding and supplies. In the spring and summer, it was used for coolness. The area around the tower would have had various paddocks to separate ewes, lambs, and yearlings, as well as numerous mangers and water troughs. Swathed lambs would have been laid in the cave and area around the tower.

The image above is the display I built to depict what Migdal Eder could have looked like on that particular night in Bethlehem. In the foreground left is the holding pen for the yearlings getting ready for the parade into Jerusalem. The middle path shows newly born lambs recently swathed by the shepherd. In the foreground right are the new moms waiting on their lambs. The cave underneath shows the manger with infant Yeshua wrapped in fine linen with His parents behind. And the watchman in the tower is diligently looking for birthing ewes and possible predators.

Lamb Selection Day in ancient Israel took place on Nisan 10. This is when the yearlings were herded up to the Jerusalem Road behind the Migdal Eder. Then, they would be led to the west gates of Jerusalem, into the city, and eventually into homes for four days. The slaughter of the lambs and Passover meal took place on Nisan 15. What modern Christianity calls the Triumphal Entry of Yeshua into Jerusalem took place on Nisan 10. How could the Chief Priests and Pharisees knowingly execute Yeshua on Nisan 15, at the same time the sacrificial lambs were slaughtered? This fulfilled Isaiah 53:7.

> *Micah 4:8 says... as for you, tower of the flock (Migdol Eder), Hill of the daughter of Zion, To you, it will come—Even the former dominion will come, The kingdom of the daughter of Jerusalem.* Another way to perceive the tower is Defender of the Flock because Migdal also means defended wall.

Where exactly was Migdal Eder located? No one is sure, but ancient writers revealed proximity to Bethlehem and Jerusalem. Published distances vary from three miles to six miles between them. However, my research points to a three-mile distance. Lightfoot, Chapter 4 Section 4, says, *from the words alleged, we infer that there was a tower or a place by the name Migdal Eder, but a very little space from Jerusalem, and that it was the situation the south side of the city...*

From Edersheim, in Sketches, paragraph 19, *We know that on the night our savior was born, the angel's message came to those who, probably alone or all in or near Bethlehem, were keeping watch. For, close by Bethlehem, on the road to Jerusalem, was a tower known as Migdal Eder, the watchtower of the flock. For here was the station where shepherds watched their flock destined for sacrifices in the Temple. So well-known was this, that if animals were found as far from Jerusalem as Migdal Eder, and within that circuit on every side, the males were offered as burnt offerings...*

Origen, p. 453 says, *Concerning the birth of Yeshua in Bethlehem...let him know that, in conformity with the narrative in the Gospel regarding His birth, there is shown at Bethlehem the cave where He was born, and the manger in the cave where He was wrapped in swaddling clothes.* This leads me to believe that Migdal Eder gave tours almost 200 years after Yeshua's time on Earth.

Flames of Faith, Glossary. *Migdal Eder is in the vicinity of Bethlehem. According to the translation of the 2nd-century sage, Yonasan ben Uziel, Migdal Eder is the place of the Messiah...*

It is important to note that at least three other Migdals are mentioned in scripture. The first is Migdal El, in the land given to Naphtali; the second is Migdal Gad, which was placed in the south of Judah, and the third was mentioned in the story of the Exodus before they passed through the Red Sea. Archeologists have recently found evidence of a tower a few miles south of Bethlehem on the road to Hebron – this might be Migdal Gad mentioned in Joshua 15:37.

From a Christian standpoint, on this holy night, the Defender of our Flock was protected by the Defender of the Flock, Migdal Eder.

V. Epilogue

The most fantastic finding during the research into the birth of the Messiah was the divine wisdom that slowly revealed itself during each phase of the project. Rhetorically, who knew about the widespread anticipation of the coming Messiah? Who was willing to take the time to investigate the actual location and meaning of the Messiah's birth? Who knew about the deep meanings of the Aramaic words in the birth story? Who knew about the Jewish roots of Christianity? Until a few years ago, I was guilty of not seeking the answer to these questions.

I eventually noticed that things didn't add up with timelines and traditions. So, I began to search and research numerous events related to anticipation and birth. The revelations and truths slowly began to unfold as each aspect was dissected. One truth led to another truth over time. But it wasn't me who was picking what to do next; God directed me, through the Holy Spirit, where to look next. It was done in His time and not mine. Matthew 7:7 is a verse that seemed to roll around in my head most often, especially when the project bogged down. The verse says...*ask, and it will be given to you; seek, and you will find; knock, and it will be opened to you*...Notice that this verse uses the verbs *ask, seek,* and *knock*, which are action words to motivate you. In a way, I'm just an obedient researcher sharing what has been given to me. What you do with this information is between you and God.

My walk with the Lord is a journey and not a destination. The subject matter in this book took place over 2000 years ago. So, what's next? There is a command in the Hebrew scriptures that we are to honor God's appointed days, called the Moedim. There are seven Moedim: the Passover, Feast of Unleavened Bread, First Fruits, Festival of Weeks, Feast of Trumpets, Day of Atonement, and the Feast of Tabernacles. Yeshua's time on earth fulfilled the first four Feasts. There are still three appointed Feasts that Yeshua has yet to fulfill: Trumpets, Atonement, and Tabernacles, in that order. With all the nonsense happening in the world today, it is time to ask, seek, and knock for God's direction so we can discern the signs of the times now, just as they were revealed to the faithful at the time of the birth.

I relate specific prophecies to road signs. As I drive on a long trip, the mileage signs are sparse, but as I get closer to my exit, the mileage signs are coming faster, and my destination gets closer. I would never stop by a road sign before I reached my destination, just like I would never link a prophecy to a specific date; it is just a road sign indicating the appointed time is approaching. Adonai doesn't want His chosen to be caught off-guard and gives us these signs for comfort and preparations. Even Luke 12:56 tells of Yeshua criticizing the Pharisees because they didn't know the signs of the times.

An excellent example of a road sign comparison happened earlier this year. It was the total eclipse that passed over the United States on April 8, 2024. It traversed America from the southwest to the northeast. The day also contained a heavenly alignment of all the moving bodies, with Mars rising first in convergence with Saturn. (Valens, at the end of Book VII, p. 137, comments that this arrangement can mean danger is ahead.) On God's calendar, it occurred on Nisan 1 -- His commanded new year. But this isn't the whole story. On August 21, 2017, a total eclipse traversed America from the northwest to the southeast, making these two eclipses crisscross the middle of the country. On God's calendar, this earlier eclipse occurred in the Hebrew month of Elul on the first day, which, in Jewish tradition, begins the daily blowing of the shofar and repentance prayers leading up to the Feast of Trumpets and Day of Atonement. Eclipses are traditionally omens of God's coming correction. Eclipses of the moon typically involve Israel; eclipses of the sun involve all the other nations. Special signs in the heavens, occurring on God's appointed days, should be taken seriously.

These are road signs, so go back to Matthew 7:7 to *ask, seek and knock*. Pray for discernment, wisdom, and peace so you can know *the signs of the times*.

VI. Appendix

Appendix 1.
More about the Passover lambs

How many lambs would have been sacrificed in Jerusalem during Passover? Josephus, Jewish War Ch 9 section 3, has this passage about Passover in 65 AD – one of the last celebrations before the Temple was destroyed. In this passage, he was trying to estimate the population in Jerusalem for the feast. *So these high priests, upon the coming of that feast which is called the Passover, when they slay their sacrifices, from the ninth hour till the eleventh, but so that a company not less than ten belong to every sacrifice, (for it is not lawful for them to feast singly by themselves,) and many of us are twenty in a company, found the number of sacrifices was two hundred and fifty-six thousand five hundred; which, upon the allowance of no more than ten that feast together, amounts to two millions seven hundred thousand....*

The Talmud, in *Pesachim 70a:10*, makes this interesting comment concerning the Passover lambs: *Come and hear: The hagigah [the lamb] which comes with the Passover is as the Passover: it comes from the flock, ... it comes from the males... it comes a year old, but it does not come a two-year-old... and it may be eaten only roasted, and it may be eaten only by those who have registered for it. The*

Scholars asked: According to the son of Tema, is it subject to the prohibition of breaking a bone, or is it not subject to the prohibition of breaking a bone? Do we say, though the Divine Law assimilated it to the Passover, yet the Writ saith, 'neither shall ye break a bone thereof...'

Appendix 2.
More about the priestly garments and the High Priest's headdress

The claim that the High Priest's headdress was used for Yeshua's swathing cloth is bold. So, it requires additional information for credibility.

Below are Talmudic and Mishnaic examples explaining that 1) the worn or soiled clothing of the priest must be salvaged as wicks for the oil lamps, 2) the worn or damaged garments of the High Priest must be buried, and 3) Priests and the High Priest must not wear their garments outside of the Temple. An unused headwrap of fine linen from the High Priest appears to uphold these guidelines.

Ibn Ezra, in Exodus 28:2:1, *And thou shalt make holy garments. They are called holy because they were worn during the sanctuary service.*

Ramban, in Leviticus 16:4, *He shall put on the linen tunic of Holiness. This means that all the garments of the High Priest must be of the treasury and not his possession. He must wear the garments in the Temple only.*

Mishnah, Torah 8:5, *Whenever any of the priestly garments become soiled, they are not to be bleached or laundered. Instead, they are left to be used as wicks... When the High Priest's garments become worn out, they should be entombed.*

Tamid 27b:5-8: *About the priestly vestments.... the one who leaves the Temple dressed...is prohibited.*

The most crucial point supporting the use of the High Priest's headdress is a word used in the Aramaic scriptures. This can be found in Luke 2:7 from "The Aramaic Scriptures.com": (read right to left)

| to swath | and Miter | firstborn | a son | and birthed |

Table #4 Translation of ancient Aramaic words in Luke 2:7

The keyword for miter above is pronounced *krak-ta-ha* and is found in Oraham, p. 238. It means swathing cloth and headdress. From *LexiLogos Syriac*, the Aramaic letter *hay* combined with the *tav* at the end of the word makes it exclamatory. It is pronounced *tah-ha*. This makes the swathing cloth unique and unusual for the situation. A few verses later, the corresponding word in Luke 2:12 is pronounced *krik,* which only means wrap. Why use a different word? My interpretation is that the angel gave the shepherds a clue about the newborn at Migdal Eder: look for the infant wrapped in fine linen, which could only have come from the treasury of the Temple.

Additionally, the word miter means *headdress of the High Priest* in multiple dictionaries such as Webster, p. 923, American Heritage, p. 841, and Collins English Dictionary online.

Appendix 3.
More on linen

According to biblegateway.com, linen is made from the flax plant. It is pulled from the roots, dried, pounded into separate fibers, and washed. Regular flax was used for curtains, clothing, and sails, among other things. Bleached flax is known as "fine linen" and is very expensive. It was used exclusively by wealthy individuals and for priestly garments in the Temple.

Fine linen is mentioned several times in scripture. Examples are in Joshua 2:6, Isaiah 19:9, Genesis 41:42, 1 Chronicles 4:21, Ezekiel 9:2, and Revelation 19:14. Even angels were dressed in fine linen, according to Revelation 19.

Appendix 4.
The connection between Yeshua's birth and death

Based on the above research, Yeshua's swathing required unused fine linen. Jewish tradition, according to Adler in the Jewish Encyclopedia, states that *...immediately* *after birth the infant was bathed, rubbed with salt, and wrapped in swaddling clothes...* from Ezekiel 16:4. The mention of salt is interesting. In Old Testament scriptures, salt is part of covenants. An example can be found in 2 Chronicles 13:5, *Do you not know that the Lord God of Israel gave the rule over Israel forever to David and his sons by a covenant of salt?* This should provide a deeper meaning to Yeshua's words in Matthew 5:13: *You are the salt of the earth...*

The section describing the manger also mentioned that it had to be newly cut from limestone. Compare this to the burial story from John 19:38-40, which states that Joseph of Arimathea and Nicodemus took Yeshua's body and bound it in linen wrappings with spices. He was crucified where there was a garden and a new tomb where no one had been laid.

Did Yeshua have spices rubbed on Him? It is plausible. From Bentorah, *Hebrew Word Study* about swaddling clothes...*after the infant was born, the umbilical cord was cut and tied...they would then sprinkle the baby with a powder from myrtle leaves. Then, rub a small amount of salt that has been finely ground...* This is interesting because myrtle is an evergreen that grows primarily in Galilee, with easy access by Joseph and Mary. Further, *The Jewish Encyclopedia*, in the section titled Myrtle, describes the myrtle's prominent use in the wedding ceremony by the bridegroom. This would add a layer of meaning to our marriage to the bridegroom Yeshua.

It is not an accident that Yeshua came into this world wrapped in fine linen and spices, laid in a cut rock, then left this world dressed in fine linen, with spices, and laid in a cut rock. The significance of this proves that Yeshua *was and is who He said He was – the Lamb of God without blemish*, born in the time of Passover and became *the perfect Lamb that was slain* in the time of Passover.

Appendix 5
Why Sukkot is not the time of the birth of Yeshua

Those who support the Sukkot birth use one verse, John 1:14, as proof that Yeshua's birth was in the autumn at the time of Sukkot. Here is the verse... *And the Word became flesh, and dwelt among us; and we saw His glory, glory as of the only Son from the Father, full of grace and truth.* The key word is *dwelt*. Fourteen out of 22 different Bible versions use the word *dwelt, dwelled, or dwelling*. Four versions use the word *lived*, two use *residence*, and only one calls it a *Tabernacle*. According to Strong's Greek Concordance, *dwelt* means *to have one's tent or tabernacle*.

Dwelt is the past tense of dwell – meaning it already happened with no future connotations. I would argue that the word dwelt means *the short time Yeshua was physically on this earth in human form*. He walked among us for 36 years as a human being -- then was crucified and resurrected in His glorified body. He won't walk among us again until after the judgment at the establishment of the Millennial

Kingdom. Please refer to Appendix 6 for information about Yeshua's age.

In Aramaic, the word used in the position dwelt is pronounced *oh-gahn*. *Oh-gahn* can mean haven, safe place, refuge, or shelter. This is far from the words tent, tabernacle, or sukkah.

And repeating Cahn's earlier words, God's appointed days must come in order. *...while this [Sukkot birth] is well-meaning and sounds nice, it would have been impossible for several reasons. First, Jesus was born in a manger, and a manger is a type of feeding trough. Also, the spiritual meaning of the Feast of Tabernacles lines up with the end times and the closing of an era, not the opening or beginning of an era. Messiah's birth, death, resurrection and second coming must come in the proper chronological order...*

Appendix 6
Priest work requirements and the birth date

The concept of two Messiahs was prominent in the first and second centuries BC—well before the birth—making the name of the Messiah irrelevant. The ancient Jews counted from 483 years (from Daniel's prophecy) to know the time of His death. They could then narrow the birthdate range as part of the anticipation. Since one of their Messiahs was going to be a priest, they knew he had to follow the laws in the Torah, Leviticus 8:25-26, about the ages for practicing priests, which was 25 to 50.

The complication for our mathematics is based on the flawed AD and BC systems. AD means *anno Domini, the year of our Lord*, and BC means *before Christ*. The idea behind this system, in 525, was to make the Messiah's birth *year one or 1 AD*. The monk counted the reign length of all the rulers back to the time of Yeshua. However, he miscounted by six years, and no one knew His birth date. So we're stuck in this system and have to deal with it. Not long ago, the terminology changed to CE (common era) and BCE (before common era) to remove Christian references from the system.

As discussed earlier, 30 AD was the time of death. Think of the AD-BC system as a continuous straight line in which the first year in AD is designated 1 AD, and the first year in BC is designated 1 BC. For example ... ← forward in time...3 AD...2 AD...1 AD...1 BC...2 BC...3 BC...and so on back in time →.

Fifty is the oldest a priest can be, so I will subtract 50 years from 30 AD, meaning I will have to use both the AD and BC numbers in a line. I will count 30 numerals on the AD side and 20 numerals on the BC side. *The answer is 20 BC, the earliest possible date Messiah could be born.* If he had been born in 21 BC, one year earlier, he wouldn't have been the High Priest in 30 AD.

I will perform the same exercise for the latest date

Messiah can be born. Twenty-five years of age from 30 AD means *the newest date of His birth was 5 AD*. If he had been born in 6 AD, one year later, he would have been too young to be a priest in 30 AD. In practical terms, the birth of the Messiah had to take place between 20 BC and 5 AD. Undoubtedly, the Temple officials would have also known this span of possible birthdates. Using the procedure above, the age of Yeshua at death was 36 (30 AD + 6 BC.) Most references differ and claim the age of 33 based on birthdates up to 1 BC and language found in Luke 3:23 that says Yeshua was about 30 when His ministry began.

The anticipation of the first-century Judeans for the Messiah's first arrival is no different from our anticipation today. We look forward to significant events like the rapture or the Second Coming. We are watching blood moons, counting Jubilee cycles, trying to figure out what the *fullness of the Gentiles* means, watching red heifers, deciphering the meaning of 666, and looking for the antichrist's name.

.

VII. Bibliography

Adler, C. and Grunwald, M., *Childbirth*, JewishEncyclopedia.com, Kopelman Foundation, 2002-2021

The *American Heritage Dictionary*, Morris, W., Editor, Houghton Mifflin Company, Boston, 1979

AstrologyWeekly.com, in the section titled *Zodiacal Signs & Countries*

Baba Kamma 80a:11, from the William Davidson Talmud (Koren-Steinsaltz), released with a CC license by Koren Publishers, 2005, from Sefaria.org.

Bedwell, W., www.studiesintheword.org, 2002

Bentorah, Chaim, *Hebrew Word Study: Swaddling Clothes* from www.chaimbentorah.com

Britannica, The Information Architects of Encyclopedia. *Artaxerxes I, Encyclopedia Britannica*, 15 February 2024, https://www.britannica.com/facts/Artaxerxes-I. Accessed 15 February 2024

Chastagner, G., and Benson, D. *The Christmas Tree: Traditions, Production, and Diseases,* Plant Health Progress, October 13, 2000

Coffman, Elesha, *Why December 25?* From an article in Christianity Today, August 8, 2008

Collins English Dictionary, www. collinsenglishdictionary.com

Dio Cassius. *Roman History, Volume V: Books 46-50.* Translated by Earnest Cary, Herbert B. Foster. Loeb Classical Library 82. Cambridge, MA: Harvard University Press, 1917.

Do It In Hebrew, online dictionary at www.doitinhebrew. com

Eastman, Mark, M.D. and Missler, Chuck, "The Creator Beyond Space and Time," Copyright 1996 The Word For Today

Edersheim, A., *Life and Times of Jesus the Messiah, 1886*, from the reprint by Eerdmans Publishing Company, 1953, Grand Rapids

Edersheim, A., *Sketches of Jewish Social Life,* London, Religious Tract Society, 1876

Epstein*, H,. The Awassi Sheep with Special Reference to Improved Dairy Type,* FAO Animal Production and Health, presented in Rome, 1985

Fein, Judith, *"Who Will Help the Good Samaritans,"* in SamaritanUpdate.com, 2008

Hohmann, Leo, "*Messianic Rabbi Reveals Christ's Birth Date,*" World Net Daily, Nov 7, 2014

Hurtado, L, *The Earliest Christian Artifacts*, William

B. Eerdmans Publishing Company, Grand Rapids, Michigan/Cambridge, U.K., 2006

Ibn Ezra, *On Exodus 28:2:1*, translated by Strickman, H, and Silver, A., Menorah Publishing, 1988-2004, from Serfaria.org.

Isaiah Scroll Verses, Translation by Professors Peter Flint (Trinity Western University, Canada) and Professor Eugene Ulrich (University of Notre Dame) in association with the Israeli Museum, http://dss. collections.imj.org.il/

JewishEncyclopedia.com, the unedited full text of the 1906 Jewish Encyclopedia, by the Executive Committee of the Editorial Board, Immanuel Low

Jewish Virtual Library, in the section titled *History & Overview of the Maccabees*, from www. jewishvirtuallibrary.org, a project of the American Israel Cooperative Enterprise, AICE

Josephus, *The New Complete works of Josephus*, translated by William Whiston, Kregal Publications, Grand Rapids, 1999

Lasson, M., *When was the Letter J Invented?* www. grammarhow.com,

Lightfoot, John, *A Commentary on the New Testament from the Talmud and Hebraica,* from Christian Classics Ethereal Library online, www.ccel.com

Marqah, *The Teaching of Marqah,* translated by John McDonald, Topermann, Berlin, 1963, pp.186-188

Meshorer, Yakov, *A Treasury of Jewish Coins,* Yad Ben-Zvi Press, Jerusalem, 2001

Mishneh Baba Kamma 7.7, from the William Davidson Talmud (Koren-Steinsaltz), released with a CC license by Koren Publishers, 2005, from Sefaria.org.

Mishneh Torah 8:5, translated by Touge, E., Jerusalem, Moznaim, Pub. 1986-2007, from Sefaria.org

Molnar, Michael, *The Star of Bethlehem - The Legacy of the Magi*, Rutgers University Press, 2000

Norris, S. D., *Unraveling the Family History of Jesus*, Pen House publishing, Sheridon, WY, pp. 151 – 166, and 534, 2020

Oraham, Alexander, *Dictionary of the Assyrian Language,* Consolidated Press, Chicago, 1943

Origen, *The Complete Works of Origen,* from Internet Archive, published 2019

Ptolemy, *Tetrabiblos*, London, Davis and Dickson, 1822, from SacredTexts.com

Ramban, *On Leviticus 16:4*, translated by Chovel, C., Shilo Pub. House, 1971-1976, from Sefaria.org

Schaefer, B., *Astrological and Historical Evaluation of*

Molnar's Solution, a research paper presented at the University of Groningen, October 2014, at a Two-Day Multi-Disciplinary Colloquium

Schoenian, Susan, *Sheep 201: a Beginners Guide to Raising Sheep,* www.sheep101.info

Strack, Hermann, German Palestine Society, interview with the Samaritan High Priest, 1887, as found in Harvest Truth Database, document R906, p. 6, https://htdb.space/index/html

Strong's Greek Dictionary, as found at www.biblehub.com, 2024

Talmud Pesachim, 27b and 70a, from the William Davidson Talmud (Koren-Steinsaltz), released with a CC license by Koren Publishers, 2005, from Sefaria.org.

Valens, V., *Anthology,* Translated by Mark T. Riley FIRST EDITION, FEBRUARY 11, 2019 SKOPJE

Webster's New World College Dictionary, 4th Edition, Agnes, M. and Guralnik, D., Editors, Wiley Publishing, 2004